ADELE

ALSO BY DANNY WHITE

Harry

Ariana

Rihanna

ADELE

TO 30 AND BEYOND
THE UNAUTHORIZED BIOGRAPHY

DANNY WHITE

Michael O'Mara Books Limited

First published in Great Britain in 2022 by
Michael O'Mara Books Limited
9 Lion Yard
Tremadoc Road
London SW4 7NQ
Copyright © Michael O'Mara Books Limited 2022

A CIP catalogue record for this book is available from the British
Library.

Papers used by Michael O'Mara Books Limited are natural, recyclable
products made from wood grown in sustainable forests. The
manufacturing processes conform to the environmental regulations of
the country of origin.

ISBN: 978-1- 78929-436-1 in hardback print format
ISBN: 978-1-78929-466-8 in trade paperback format
ISBN: 978-1-78929-444-6 in ebook format

1 2 3 4 5 6 7 8 9 10
Cover Design by Natasha Le Coultre
Designed and typeset by D23
Front cover image: Alexi/Alamy Stock Photo
Back cover image: Invision/AP/Shutterstock
Printed and bound by CPI Group (UK) Ltd, Croydon, CR0 4YY
www.mombooks.com

CONTENTS

INTRODUCTION

When Adele abruptly cancelled a string of Las Vegas shows in 2022, the news made headlines around the world. Even at a time of global crisis, it still became a major story. For days, the saga was discussed in newspapers and on television. People portrayed Adele as a 'diva' who had let down her fans. One question kept being asked: what had happened to that down-to-earth girl from Tottenham?

The majesty of Adele's voice is clearly central to her appeal, but so is how relatable she is. Even the most dedicated fans of the likes of Rihanna, Katy Perry and Lady Gaga cannot seriously believe that their superstar heroes are the same as them, but if you are a fan of Adele it's often because she seems, to borrow the title of her biggest hit, someone like you.

When she emerged into the public eye, pop was a scene where many of the most successful female acts focused on their sexuality as much as their music. For instance, in 'S&M'

by Rihanna, the Barbadian sang that 'Sticks and stones may break my bones but chains and whips excite me.' Christina Aguilera, another popular act at the time, also had a very sexualized image, while Madonna and Lady Gaga had drawn criticism from within and without the industry for their heavily sexualized videos and performances. Even boys were presented this way: One Direction's Harry Styles was carefully branded as a lothario while he was still a teenager.

When Adele arrived and focused on her voice rather than her body, many felt she was a breath of fresh air. Commentators said she could strike a blow for the sisterhood in society in general by showing that women could become famous by being respected rather than lusted after. Then there was her weight: how powerful was it for young girls to see a young woman ruling the pop scene despite not having a pop-thin physique? She was always very clear that she was more than comfortable in her own skin and that her weight was simply not an issue for her. As she told *Vogue* magazine: 'Fans are encouraged that I'm not a size zero – that you don't have to look a certain way to do well.'

She told us she preferred drinking cider in the park with her mates to hanging out with A-listers at private clubs. She swore and cackled during interviews and between songs on stage. She might have sounded like Ella Fitzgerald when she sang, but when she spoke she was more like a girl sitting on the top deck of a bus. The combination of a divine voice with a down-to-earth character made Adele enormously compelling: we wowed at her talent and related to her personality. 'I think I remind people of themselves,' she said.

Did other mononymous stars, such as Prince, Madonna, or Elvis, have this same, everyman appeal?

Her material, too, has universal application. Adele has the emotional agility of a West End leading lady and sings about something every adult has experienced: a broken heart. Everyone can feel the pain in her songs, from a teenage boy suffering his first heartbreak, to a septuagenarian who has just lost her third failed marriage. This is why her star shone so bright: she was one of us and she was bringing artistic clarity to emotions we had all felt.

So, for many of her admirers, it felt like she had broken their hearts when, in 2022, she cancelled the twenty-four shows of her residency at the Caesars Palace Colosseum, just twenty-four hours before the opening date. Almost immediately there were suggestions that she had become a 'diva', and people wondered how the shy, down-to-earth girl from Tottenham had seemingly become an out-of-touch show-business celebrity.

How did Adele transform from this shy girl from north London, who liked boozing in the park with her mates, to the globally famous megastar who cancelled Vegas residencies? By telling her story, this book is an attempt to find out.

CHAPTER ONE

EARLY DAYS

After Adele became a mother in 2012, she spoke about how motherhood meant she had to make sacrifices. 'I lost a lot of myself,' she said.

Her own mother knows all about the sacrifices of parenthood. Penny Adkins had it all planned out. She was eighteen, studying at an art college in Barnet, north London, and preparing to move to university. When a lot of people are eighteen they haven't yet devised a plan for their future, preferring to simply bumble along day to day, but often this is a sign of privilege – they can afford to be that indecisive thanks to the ever-present safety net of the fabled 'bank of mum and dad'. Penny was in a very different position: she had to have a plan for her future because she had recently been asked to leave the family home – her parents believed strongly that their children must learn to make their own way in life. So Penny couldn't meander around or take a stereotypical 'gap year' to 'find herself'. She had to get motoring right away and support herself. How would she make her way in life? With creativity flowing through her veins, the artist's way seemed the right one for Penny.

Adele's mother-to-be was a tall and slim young woman, with raven-black hair. She lived in Islington, north London, having grown up near the old Arsenal football stadium, in a family with plenty of fans of the famous football club. However, she did not have a London accent and, as Adele's father remembered, no one would ever guess that Penny came from the capital. On the other hand, her looks made her stand out, he said, thanks to her 'legs up to her neck'.

A creative soul, she loved to draw and paint, or play her guitar. She hoped that her plans to take up an art course might help her make her way along a creative path. The thought of making a living out of her love of creating things excited Penny. Then, her plans went awry when she discovered she was pregnant. Little could she have known that the child she was expecting would go down that creative path herself, and become a globally recognized artist.

Penny's life took this unexpected diversion after she met a Welshman called Marc Evans in a north London pub. She was in her teens, but Evans was in his mid-twenties when they met. Evans, a broadly built window cleaner, also had the gift of the gab and the looks to go with his charm. They met on a fateful evening in the summer of 1987 at The King's Head in Crouch End, north London. They got chatting and quickly hit it off, so they arranged a second date, this time at a more central venue. Marc's favourite pub was the eighteenth-century Punch and Judy in Covent Garden, so they arranged to meet there. He realized that

Penny was not the sort of young woman he would be able to rush into the bedroom, but they kept meeting at the pub. As he explained to the author Sean Smith, the Punch and Judy quickly became 'their place'.

It was in 'their place' that Penny first dropped the big bombshell news and told Evans that she was pregnant. He was shocked, to say the least, but tried to present a composed and supportive face for the expectant mother. Just a week later, at the same trusty boozer, he did the 'decent thing' and asked Penny to marry him. He felt that he was doing the right thing by Penny, but she actually turned him down, telling him they were far too young to tie the knot. Whether Marc was secretly relieved is not known.

So she was not to marry, but she did have to make changes to her life. She gave up her dream of a college course but, in keeping with the family philosophy, she still left home, moving into emergency accommodation for unmarried mothers in Finsbury Park. Glamorous it was certainly not, but she was supported by the National Childbirth Trust charity, which has helped millions of parents through birth and early parenthood since it was founded in 1956.

On 5 May 1988, Penny's baby was still two weeks away from her due date but, in contrast to most musical divas who infamously arrive late for all engagements, this one decided to arrive early. Adele was born at North Middlesex Hospital, weighing 5 pounds, 10.5 ounces. Her date of birth makes Adele a Taurus. Like her celestial spirit animal, she has guts aplenty but appreciates a sense of stability and comfort. Some say Taureans like to be in control and, as we shall see, Adele was not un-controlling when it came to her career. Indeed, it was the things she was not able to control that freaked her out about it all.

Penny and Marc disagreed over what name to choose for their new girl. Marc wanted to call her Blue, but Penny gave that idea very short shrift. She preferred the name Adele, but she added two middle names: Laurie and, as a gesture to Marc, Blue. When Marc began to nevertheless refer to his new daughter as Blue, Penny would tick him off and remind him what her real first name was.

Life in Finsbury Park was hard so Penny was pleased when she was rehoused from the emergency accommodation into a two-bedroom council flat in Tottenham. Marc helped her settle in and would sometimes stay over at the flat with them. After a month he moved in officially. Penny felt more settled and safer there, but there was no hiding from the fact that her life had been turned upside down. Just months earlier she was living at home in Islington and preparing to start a new course, embarking in search of her artistic dreams. Now, she was a mother living in a council flat in Tottenham.

None of this sacrifice and upheaval is lost on Adele today. She is only too mindful that Penny fell pregnant with her when she was planning to go to university but 'chose to have me instead'. The singer adds that her mother 'never, ever reminds me of that' but that, nevertheless, she tries to remember it to honour her mother's love. Indeed, Adele fondly remembers many parts of her childhood. She has recalled trips to south Wales, when Marc and Penny would take her to see her paternal grandparents. She loved the knickerbocker glory dessert treats and the family walks along the promenade in Penarth. These were idyllic moments, but within months of her birth, any spark between Marc and Penny was extinguished. When Adele was just nine months old the couple split. Penny would be, essentially, raising Adele alone, though she came from a big clan, so was not without a support structure.

'There was never any embarrassment about showing love in my family,' said Adele of that structure, noting that she had around thirteen cousins living in and around the Tottenham area. That scale of family must have helped Adele feel grounded, and also gave her lots of opportunities for people-watching, an essential tool in any songwriter's toolkit. If you want to convey a range of human emotions convincingly in art, you have to have been exposed to those emotions over and over, and in an uncensored form. But there was one thing that marked Adele out from most children, a thing that would guide the path she eventually took, and with so much success. At the tender age of three, she became fascinated with people's voices and how those voices reflected their moods. 'I used to listen to how the tones would change from angry to excited to joyful to upset,' she said. This points to a household where, as well as there being no embarrassment over showing love, there was no shame in expressing your emotions.

Music, naturally, became part of all this expression, and its importance in her childhood can hardly be overstated. Although surrounded by relatives, Adele lacked a direct sibling and could also, like most children, sometimes feel she lacked human companionship. Therefore, music became very important to her. 'It was my friend,' she told *Vogue*. 'Music was literally my friend. I was an only child. Music was my sibling I never had. That's why I love Beyoncé so much. She would put out music so regularly, it would be like seeing her. It really felt like that for me. It made me feel a lot of things.' To consider Beyoncé, and music itself, as her friends, shows how intimate and passionate she was.

She also noticed other things about music, including that it moved people 'and I loved the feeling of that,' she said. Her ears were taking in plenty of shaping sounds because among Adele's earliest memories are the concerts Penny took her to. She was being introduced to live music at an extraordinarily young age. The first concert was of the The Cure, at nearby Finsbury Park. This post-punk band, fronted by the make-up-wearing Robert Smith, was not the sort of act many children would be aware of, let alone go to see live. Also on the bill that day was Damon Albarn of Blur. Adele was just five years old when she saw him perform. Two decades later their paths would cross professionally, but not in the most harmonious way. On the other hand, her love of The Cure would emerge happily and gloriously in one of her own releases.

Penny also managed to smuggle young Adele into another concert: The Beautiful South at Brixton Academy. She hid her daughter in her coat to get her through the ticket checks at the door of the vast south London venue. 'It was an amazing gig, really raucous but really fantastic,' said Adele later. 'I was so little I couldn't see anything, but there was a bodybuilder standing near us, so my mum just put me on his shoulders, and then I could see perfectly.' When balloons were released Adele didn't manage to grab one at first. For a child such moments can be painfully disappointing, but the bodybuilder gallantly 'knocked someone out' so Adele could have one, she remembered. She ranks that evening as the 'clearest memory' of her childhood, growing up with her 'hippy mum', whom she adored.

More experiences with live music were to come, with Adele collecting quite a pile of ticket stubs for a girl her age. At the age of six she went to see the London boy band East 17. (She saw the band again, twelve years later, when they reformed for a concert at Shepherd's Bush Empire – 'best gig, ever', she told *Q* magazine.) Penny also took her daughter to the Glastonbury Festival, where they saw a number of acts, including Prodigy and Radiohead. On Friday nights, Penny would allow Adele to stay up until the heady hour of quarter past eleven in the evening to watch the BBC's flagship live music show, *Later … with Jools Holland*. The range of artists who were booked for *Later* and the live shows she was being taken to all ensured that Adele was getting a broad spectrum of sounds. Many girls and boys Adele's age would have been tucked up in bed by this late hour, but Adele was wide awake, absorbing so much about music.

Penny tried to support and nurture whatever her daughter's interests were at any stage. Adele expressed interest in several paths, including playing the saxophone, becoming a fashion correspondent, a ballet dancer or a weather girl. Like a lot of kids, her interest in these ambitions could come and go in a flash. One moment it would seem like a matter of life and death that she got that saxophone or took those dance classes, and the next moment she would have forgotten about them, because a new interest had captured her imagination. Penny always aimed to support them. Adele said her mother always told her: 'Do what you want, and if you're happy, I'm happy.' Rather than jealously resenting Adele's interest in creativity, after her birth diverted her own ambitions in that direction, Penny lovingly encouraged her daughter. She was less focused on what she had lost by becoming a mother, and more interested in what she had gained.

She sent Adele to the Coleraine Park Primary School, an ethnically mixed establishment. There, her child got a reputation as someone who stood up to bullies and protected her friends. This garnered her a degree of respect and credibility. Adele was also a generous girl, who would always share any sweets she had. Music continued to rule, though, and before she was even a teenager she would queue for hours to get into recordings of Saturday morning show *CD:UK*. This ITV show, a rival of the BBC's *Live & Kicking*, broadcast live on Saturday mornings with a studio audience and live performances, as well as star interviews and competitions. Adele enjoyed morning television programmes. As a fan also of *Live & Kicking* she became a huge fan of the presenter, Zoe Ball. 'She was just brilliant,' said Adele. 'When she got married and got out of that car in a wedding dress holding a bottle of Jack Daniels, that was it for me. That was how I wanted to be. And I was only little.'

Actually, Adele, now a hero to millions, had many heroes as a child. At school she pretended to have an eye injury to justify wearing a sequinned eye-patch in honour of the pop singer Gabrielle. She got teased and went off the accessory. The diva was not her only pop idol; she also loved Mike Skinner, the singer behind the urban act The Streets, who became famous for tracks such as 'Dry Your Eyes' and 'Fit but You Know It'. Her devotion was a vulnerable force, as she remembered later in life. 'I was so in love with Mike Skinner I wrote him a letter, and when I told my friend about it she cussed me so I went and pretended to do the washing up and cried,' she said.

However, one of the most profound influences on her was the Spice Girls, whom she discovered at the age of ten. 'Even though some people think they're uncool, I'll never be ashamed to say I love the Spice Girls because they made me who I am,' she said. 'I got into music right in their prime when they were huge. They're the reason I wanted to be an entertainer. Obviously they're not great singers and I knew that when I was seven. But what they did was amazing.'

Among those who thought the girl band uncool was Adele's father, Marc. Not once to mince his words, he said he thought them 'bloody awful'.

Nevertheless, the impact they had on his daughter was clear and undiminished. 'It was a huge moment in my life when they came out,' she said. 'It was girl power. It was five ordinary girls who did so well and just got out. I was like, I want to get out.' Her favourite member was Geri initially. 'I just remember seeing Geri and being, like: "Fuck it, I'm going to do that. I want to be Ginger Spice."' However, many Spice Girls fans change their favourite over time. Adele was no different, and her favourite member would soon be Scary Spice herself, Mel B.

As well as enjoying the generally upbeat and superficial pop of the Spice Girls, Adele loved deeper and sadder songs. For instance, the first track that ever made her cry was Sinéad O'Connor's song 'Troy'. It is a haunting tune. Although more Gaelic-sounding than Adele's style, lyrically it is not a million miles from the music Adele would make. Its nostalgic bent brings to mind the tone and theme of her third album, 25.

Adele was very much on the road to becoming a pop star herself, right from the age of five. When Penny had dinner parties she would ask Adele to stand on the table and sing. A regular track was 'Dreams', by Gabrielle. The track seems fitting for Adele's musical ambition, with its message that dreams can come true. Adele also tackled another Gabrielle song, 'Rise'. But this time it was at a more public venue: her school.

Adele's love of music was being spotted. Her father had noticed his daughter's talent – and he also claims a share of the credit for it. 'I'd lie on the sofa all night, cradling Adele in my arms and listening to my favourite music – Ella Fitzgerald, Louis Armstrong, Bob Dylan and Nina Simone. Night after night, I'd play those records. I'm certain that is what shaped Adele's music,' he told the *Daily Mail*. He remembers that she came to stay when she was just seven years of age carrying a little acoustic guitar she'd picked up in a charity shop. She had wanted to play her mother's full-size guitar but it was just too big for her to master at this stage. 'She said she was teaching herself how to play it by listening to the blues songs we used to listen to on my record player and then trying to make the same noise,' said Marc.

Within a couple of years, she was also singing along. A key album in her development was *The Miseducation of Lauryn Hill*. It was played constantly in the house and Adele sat with the lyric sheet, singing along. 'I remember having the sleeve notes and reading every lyric and not understanding half of them and just thinking: "When am I going to be that passionate about something to write a record about it?"' she said in an interview quoted by *People* magazine. Penny challenged her daughter and encouraged her to dig deeper. She asked Adele if she understood the song's words. This helped Adele analyse and absorb music more deeply, nurturing the connection and understanding between words and music that is so necessary for someone to become a songwriter themselves. She grew to love the more urban sound of acts like Lauryn Hill, Faith Evans and Mary J. Blige.

Hero after hero: Adele was also a big fan of Beyoncé at this stage – and still is. 'She's been a huge and constant part of my life as an artist since I was about ten or eleven,' she said. 'I love how all her songs are about empowerment.' Adele said she would try and sound like Beyoncé as she sang Destiny's Child songs. At the age of 'thirteen or fourteen' Adele discovered the music of Pink. 'I had never heard, being in the room, someone sing like that live,' she said of the solo star. 'I remember sort of feeling like I was in a wind tunnel, her voice just hitting me. It was incredible.' A reviewer for that very show observed that 'fame alone doesn't do it for Pink – she really wants to mean something'.

The more Adele sang, the better she became. The better she became, the more people sat up and took notice of her – even as a child her ascendancy was mirroring that of a professional. 'I remember thinking, when she was seven, my God, Adele's really got it,' Marc told the *Mail on Sunday*. 'She's going to be a huge star one day.' However, Adele does not go along happily with the suggestion that her talent was somehow inevitable. 'People think that I popped out of my mother's womb singing "Chasing Pavements",' she said, according to *Adele: The Biography*. She does not agree that she was born to perform. 'Fuck off, no one's born to perform,' she said.

Meanwhile, her musical education was continuing. She started playing the clarinet around the age of eleven and reached grade five, but then 'when I started smoking, I couldn't play no more', she told *The Attic* online magazine. She took up the fags when she was around thirteen, she recalled. She also played the saxophone as a child and began playing the guitar at the age of seventeen. Her dad bought her a Simon & Patrick guitar, an instrument later admired by Who guitarist Pete Townshend when he met Adele.

With her love of music building, she had what the *Observer* newspaper described as a 'dog-collared American rock phase', that would see her regularly browsing the shelves of her local HMV music and film shop for Korn and Slipknot CDs, 'a little forlorn in her baggy jeans and not quite sure it was the fad for her'. It was during one such visit to the record store that she noticed a record by Etta James. Initially, it was the singer's haircut that Adele noticed. She also liked the energy emitting from James's face. 'You wouldn't want to mess with her, she was so fucking fierce,' Adele said. This moment planted a seed in her mind that has emerged through her own releases.

There is little doubt who Adele's favourite act is. 'She's my favourite singer ever,' she said of Etta James. 'She's got the richest voice in the world.' However, Adele nearly never discovered that voice. Having bought the James CD, she promptly lost it under a pile of stuff in her room. 'Then one day I was clearing out my room and I found it and put it on,' she said. 'When I heard the song "Fool That I Am", everything changed for me. I never wanted to be a singer until I heard that.'

Like a lot of teenagers, Adele went through various looks and styles. They were mostly influenced by street trends. 'From twelve to thirteen I was a grunger,' she said. 'Criminal Damage jeans. Dog collars. Hoodies. We used to go to

Camden all the time because we were, like, "so dark". Then I really got into R&B and became a rude girl – in Adidas, with a spit curl! Tiny Nike backpacks. Mine was black, with a logo bigger than the bag.'

She needed money for all these clothes, CDs and instruments, so Adele took various jobs. One was working in a café which her auntie ran in Haringey, north London. Adele worked on Sundays when the pop charts would be announced over the radio. 'It was really shit pay and long hours but it was the most fun I ever had,' she said. She also worked in the clothing store, Gap. Here, the pay was better, but the work was much less fun. She had imagined herself working on the tills or by the changing rooms, but the reality was hour upon hour of folding jumpers. 'It was so boring I walked out after four days,' she said.

Reality television was far more interesting to her. *Pop Idol* captivated the nation when it first appeared on ITV in 2001. Although a previous pop talent series, *Popstars*, had captured the imagination with its search for the pop band that became Hear'Say, *Pop Idol* took things to a new height, not least because of its outspoken judge, Simon Cowell. Barely heard of outside the music industry before the talent series, he quickly became a household name thanks to his brutally honest verdicts.

In series one of *Pop Idol*, the hopefuls were eventually whittled down to two clear favourites: Gareth Gates and

Will Young. It was a strong final two, which has arguably never been matched on any subsequent reality pop series. Gates had the boy band looks, but posh Young had a wider charisma and wit. It felt like almost everyone in the nation had a favourite out of the two. Adele was very much in the Will camp – so much so that she got into a fight one day as she defended her favourite's honour.

It all kicked off among her schoolmates, who were clearly divided between the two finalists. 'The Gareth Gates fans were horrible to me and I wasn't having any of it,' she told the *Sunday Mirror*. 'We had a fight and I was called into the head teacher's office and sent home. It was serious.' However, she had the last laugh and she must have been delighted when Young won the series final, upsetting the widespread predictions that Gates would absolutely romp home.

Gripped as she was by the *Pop Idol* series and enchanted as she was by Young, Adele did not see the talent show route as her path to fame. 'You've got all their parents, and they're like "Yeah she's the next Whitney, the next Mariah,"' she said, 'and then they go on and they're shit.' The judges on *Pop Idol* may have been harsh with their judgements, but the misguided hope that contestants were given by their parents did not sit well with Adele. It even made her doubt the praise that her own mother would give her. (Not that any of this could diminish her love of Young. When she met him several years later she was so excited she blurted out: 'I voted for you 5,000 times!')

She also found the Mariah Carey impersonators on the show a bit much, with their overly showy and warbling delivery. 'So many people sing like that now, and I could do it if I wanted to, but the first time you hear it you're like, wow, and by the fifth time, it's like f*** off, get something new,' she told the *Daily Telegraph*. 'It's more impressive, somehow, if you don't try to impress. Be natural with it. Say it straight.' Perhaps, with this nurturing and advisory nature, Adele could be a judge on a talent show in the future. Her mixture of outspoken sassiness and maternal caring would be a strong blend, but she wouldn't come cheap.

Meanwhile, there were a few upheavals on the cards for Adele. When she was nine, Penny moved them to Brighton on England's south coast, where she took a job at a furniture store. They lived in East Drive, near Queen's Park. The atmosphere at the seaside town can feel idyllic and creative to many, but Adele was not a fan. 'The people seemed really pretentious and posh and there were no black people there,' she told *The Times*, remembering how she had missed the more urban surroundings she was used to. 'I was used to being the only white kid in my class in Tottenham.' Within two years they were back in London, albeit the southern outskirts, as they moved to a flat in West Norwood.

Another change came when Adele's father had a son, Cameron, with a new partner. Sometimes children are upset when a half-sibling arrives on the scene but not Adele. She was thrilled that Cameron came into her life. After all; she had previously been pretending Beyoncé was her sibling –

now she had a real one. 'He looks like my twin,' she said in an interview quoted in the *Daily Mail*. 'We're identical, same hair and everything.' She said that, although they grew up in different cities, she and Cameron were as close as if they lived together. She admitted she would bully him, but only in the way elder siblings often do. She actually grew to love the contrast between her visits to Marc's new family, when she had a younger sibling to have fun with, and her life back in London, when she enjoyed the advantages of being the only child. 'It was like the best of both worlds,' she said.

Adele was showing a skill for looking on the positive side of what life threw at her, but some things are hard to perceive in a positive way. Her first heartbreak came when her paternal grandfather, John, died. Adele remembered how he loved Penny and considered her a daughter because Evans was not a constant presence. 'I think my dad was Adele's most significant role model,' Evans told the *Daily Mail*. 'They spent a lot of time together, just the two of them.' As for Adele, she said she 'painted' John as a 'Jesus figure in my life'.

She was ten years old when John was diagnosed with bowel cancer and admitted to the Velindre Cancer Centre in Cardiff. Adele remembered visiting him in hospital and the defence mechanism she adopted to cope, reported the *Daily Star*. 'I was so uncomfortable with it that I nicked his wheelchair and was just going up and down the hospital corridors because I couldn't face the fact that the love of my life, my granddad, was dying.' Looking back, she wishes she spent more time at his bedside, telling him she loved him, but for a girl of ten to not know how to handle such a testing and traumatic situation is no crime.

John died within weeks of his admission, at the age of fifty-seven. Adele attended the funeral service at the Tabernacle Baptist Church in Penarth. 'I was so sad,' she remembered. She was so distraught, in fact, that Penny sought bereavement counselling for her daughter within weeks of the service. 'I've been in and out of therapy since I was a kid,' she told *The Face* magazine later. Adele said the experience of losing her grandfather shaped her attitude towards religion. 'I'm not religious myself, but I appreciate religion so deeply because when my grandpa died, I don't think my nana would've got through it without her faith, so the comfort that religion gives people I've got all day long for,' she said.

By her father's own account, he did not offer Adele sufficient comfort at this time. He has admitted to being a 'rotten father' and said he is 'deeply ashamed' that he was not there for her as she grieved. He took this shame to his grave, but at the time he was suffering from a double bereavement: he had lost both his father and a friend, who had died of a heart attack. It would have been nice for a father to support his daughter at a time of a family crisis but, again, it is not the gravest of offences to have been distant at a time he was going through so much himself.

Evans once said that Adele's songs are 'rooted in the very dark places she went through as a young girl'. He regards John's death as one of these dark places, but there was also much happiness during those years, thanks in part to the love and sacrifices of her mother. As we have seen, Adele has been obsessed with people's voices since childhood. During those formative years, Penny's voice was a soundtrack of support. Adele's arrival had somewhat derailed Penny's artistic dreams, but she responded by encouraging her daughter in her exploration of music. That exploration saw Adele switch schools midway through her secondary years, moving to a haven of creativity. Penny might not have made it to art school but her daughter would.

CHAPTER TWO

FINDING HER PASSION

When she was fourteen, Adele applied to join the BRIT School, the UK's first free performing and creative arts school for people aged fourteen to nineteen. In her application she said that she was 'someone who is dedicated to music purely through love and passion for it'. She added that she wanted to 'build on my songwriting both musically and lyrically'. She hoped, she added, that she would 'keep trying until I am completely satisfied with what I have created'. These were fine and ambitious words for a girl in her early teens, and the tone of perfectionism will be recognized with a wry smile by those who have subsequently worked with her on her albums.

Adele's move to the BRIT School had in its roots her dissatisfaction with her then establishment, Chestnut Grove. Although it specialized in visual arts and therefore some might hope it had a creative energy in its air, Adele felt her school in Balham lacked ambition. 'I hated the school I was at, I was at a normal school and didn't like it,' she said. This lack of ambition had clearly upset her deeply. She later told *The Times* that the teachers 'didn't really encourage' her. She complained that whether she told them she wanted to be a musician or to be a heart surgeon, their response would be, effectively, 'try and finish school and don't get pregnant'. As she put it later, 'things were looking quite bleak'. She remembered being 'mouthy' and playing truant, playing up because she was unhappy with her lot. 'The only reason I ended up studying music at the BRIT School was because I knew I was going to fail all my GCSEs, so I panicked,' she told *Fabulous* magazine.

After teachers at her school tried to make her play clarinet in order to be allowed to sing in the choir, it felt like the last straw had been reached. Adele was desperate to move to a school that she felt would encourage her creativity in a more straightforward way. The only question was where she would go next. Initially, she wanted to attend the legendary Sylvia Young Theatre School in central London, not least because Emma Bunton (a.k.a. Baby Spice from the Spice Girls) went there. Among its other famous alumni are Amy Winehouse, Billie Piper and Denise Van Outen. Adele would have loved to join that list. 'But my mum couldn't afford it,' she told *Q*. Remembering her disappointment, she said: 'I was bitter and twisted.'

Instead, she ended up at the BRIT School, which was, according to one of its teachers, Dec Cunningham, 'basically a local comprehensive'. However, another teacher said that the beauty of the BRIT School is that is designed for 'the non-type'. They added: 'The school fits round their personality, rather than asking them to form their personality round the school.' This seems very fitting for Adele. The school had been launched after a fundraising concert at Knebworth House on 30 June 1990. An estimated 120,000-strong audience flocked to the Hertfordshire park on a windy Saturday to hear slots from the likes of Pink Floyd, Phil Collins and Tears For Fears. The event helped raise initial funds to construct the school, and a year later, in 1991, the BRIT School opened in Croydon, south London.

When she attended an open day ten years later, Adele was shown round by a student called Beverly Tawiah. The student really inspired Adele, who remembered later: 'She really encouraged me and she was a brilliant singer. I thought: "That's it, I'm coming here."' When it came to her audition interview, Adele found herself in front of the deputy head of music, Liz Penney. The thirteen-year-old Adele sang the Stevie Wonder track 'Free'. She was also required to play a song on a musical instrument and chose to perform 'Tumbledown Blues' by James Rae on the clarinet. Asked why she thought she should be given a place at the school, Adele said: 'Because I'm creative.' Penney remembered, 'When she opened her mouth to sing, I thought: "Well, that's a larger voice than you would expect from a thirteen year old."'

In his book *Adele*, Sean Smith writes that 'on any given morning, commuters waiting on platform 1 at the overground station in West Norwood would see a young teenager in a Goth studded collar and parachute pants giving her full concentration to *Heat* magazine or the latest edition of *i-D*, the style bible for modern youth culture'. She would have slept in and usually arrived late, getting in trouble with the teachers, recalled fellow pupil Ben Thomas, who would go on to become her guitarist. In a slight contradiction of Adele's account of her feelings at her previous school, Thomas also told *Rolling Stone* magazine that she lacked ambition, at least in comparison to some of the students there. 'There were some people at school who really pushed hard,' he said. 'You could tell they really wanted it. Adele never had that.' However, Liz Penney did notice ambition. 'Her drive to be a songwriter was evident quite early on. We'd often see her outside in the corridor; writing lyrics; picking up the guitar and learning how to accompany herself.'

As for Adele, she just remembered her tardiness. 'I'd turn up to school four hours later. I was sleeping. I wasn't bunking. I just couldn't wake up,' she told *Rolling Stone*. She had moments of self-doubt. 'I never thought my being a professional singer was going to happen, so I sometimes thought it was a waste of time pursuing something that most likely was not going to happen,' she said. She also felt that the teachers sometimes dissected music a little too forensically. 'I don't want to do that,' she said. She had a wake-up call – quite literally – when she missed a trip to perform at a festival in Devon. It had been arranged for some of the BRIT's most promising pupils and she was supposed to be there, but, once again, she overslept and missed out. She discovered the news when her phone rang.

'My heart exploded in my chest,' she remembered. 'It was pretty horrible. I almost did get kicked out of school for that.' This would not be the last time in her life that she would miss a scheduled performance.

However, for all her naughtiness, her talent soon began to stand out a mile. At one morning assembly – to which she managed to arrive on time – she sang a song that impressed Stuart Worden, who later became the headmaster, so much he asked if he could have a copy. Her reply was pure Adele sass: 'Well …' she said, 'you'll have to buy it.' The creative energy of the school was encouraging and inspiring her in just the way she had hoped it would. 'Whereas before I was going to a school with bums and kids that were rude and wanted to grow up and mug people,' she told *Blues & Soul* magazine, 'it was really inspiring to wake up every day to go to school with kids that actually wanted to be productive at something and wanted to be somebody.'

So whereas the kids 'doing pirouettes in the fucking hallway' were clearly memorable and a bit irritating for Adele, she was happy at a school 'full of kids that will dance at a freezing-cold town hall barefoot for eight hours solid'. She was able to see how the good outweighed the bad, a strong perspective for a girl in her teens. 'It was a bit like *Fame*

sometimes – you get people doing their ballet stretches and singers having sing-offs,' she told the *News of the World*, but added, tellingly: 'I'd rather that than someone pulling a knife!'

As well as balance, she was also showing she had self-awareness. 'If I hear someone's from stage school I'd think they were a dickhead, and I know it might make me sound like that,' she told the *Independent*. 'But it had free rehearsal rooms and free equipment and I was listening to music all day, every day, for years. The music course was really wicked. There was no dancing or anything like that. No jazz hands.' Not that she was romantic about every pupil; she thought some of her fellow students were actually going backwards. 'Some of the people there are atrocious, really bad,' she remembered. 'They all wanna be fucking soul singers! I'm all up for people who are in development, but not people who are in there for four years and start when they're shit and leave when they're even worse.'

Among the pupils who were better when they left was the pop singer Kate Nash, who Adele remembers as always doing impressions and 'so funny'. Another famous alumnus was Katie Melua, who Adele recalls as 'lovely' and with a 'wicked voice'. Katy B, who also attended the BRIT School, said of our heroine: 'Having people like Adele pass around knowledge and information and being so passionate about what you are learning is amazing'.

Jessie J, who became an award-winning, chart-topping singer, said of her time at the BRIT School that Adele was 'the girl everyone loved and up for a laugh'. She added that

'You could hear her laugh from a mile down the corridor.' Another now-famous singer who was at the BRIT School then was Leona Lewis, but Adele cannot remember her. 'That Leona Lewis must've been a quiet horse as I can't remember her at all,' said Adele. Revealing the sort of friendly and observant character she herself was back then, Adele added: 'And I knew everyone there.'

The fact that Adele once studied there is a colossal feather in the cap for the BRIT School. To this day, new students cite this as their inspiration for applying to join and for working diligently once they arrived. In 2017, singing student Alice Mead-Bishop, eighteen, told the BBC that Adele's success motivated her. 'Being able to have so many amazing people who have come here is so admirable and inspiring,' she said.

As for Adele, she is clear on the part that her teachers played in her musical development. It was not all about the music itself. 'Nobody at the BRIT School taught me how to sing,' she told the BBC, looking back. 'I taught me how to sing listening to Etta James at home. What they taught me was how the business works.' Indeed they did. She learned how to use a recording studio, including how to soundcheck microphones, amplifiers and speaker systems. 'It's handy, 'cause you don't have to pay people to do it for you.' She also brushed up on how contracts and budgets work, and other things that many artists know little about. 'Most artists haven't got a clue,' she told *The Times*, later. 'They get me to sign contracts now and it's a big joke, it's like, "Do you understand this long word written down here, Adele?" And I'm like: "Yes, I do actually. It means you're trying to rip me off."' She became a music moneyman's worst nightmare – and all the better for it.

These were happy and helpful times for Adele. 'A lot of people feel trapped by youth, but at BRIT I felt fucking alive,' she said. 'They taught us to be open-minded and we were really encouraged to write our own music – and some of us took that seriously and some of us didn't. I took it very seriously.' When she was touring America in 2011, she was told that she had made music history because her second album had been at Number One for an unprecedented ten weeks. 'Thanks to the BRIT School,' she remarked. It felt important for her to always remember and acknowledge where she came from. Adele's gratitude for the place can best be summed up in a single sentence from her during an interview with the *News of the World*: 'I hate to think where I'd have ended up if I hadn't gone.'

'Everyone was telling me to write songs and I just did it for fun,' remembered Adele about the early days of her career. 'I was being a bit stubborn without knowing and didn't want to write any. I didn't have time, I was being a lady of leisure, going out to parties.' There was a danger that she would become another of those potential songwriters who just cannot break past their aspirations and turn them into reality.

But a boyfriend was to prove the spark that lit the flame that has burned ever since. 'And then I got my heart broken and the whole album's about that. I am grateful. I hate him but I am grateful.'

Perhaps a major talent like Adele would have found her way into the music industry one way or another, but while she can thank her ex for the inspiration for her first album, she can thank Lily Allen and Amy Winehouse for the big break that got her that record deal in the first place. Allen had shown that the social networking site Myspace could be an effective way to promote your music. In 2005, she was a pop hopeful with a sizeable Myspace following, and within a few years she was a hit singer. In what felt like the flick of a coin, she went from an unknown to a nationally famous, much-loved star, with tracks such as 'Smile', 'The Fear' and 'Fuck You'.

As for Winehouse, she, like Allen, had helped to create an appetite for sassy young female acts. Once those two had shown that female solo singers with plenty of attitude could reach the top of the charts and bank millions, the record industry was naturally on the lookout for the next one. Adele would soon hit their radar. And yet this link-up could quite easily never have existed, because Adele initially had other plans. When she graduated from the BRIT School, she saw her future in the music industry. However, she did not imagine herself on stage but in the behind-the-scenes role of A&R. Standing for Artists and Repertoire, it is the part of the team that is responsible for talent scouting and the development of recording artists. The A&R man – it is still a sector dominated by men – also acts as a liaison between the artist and the record label.

'I wanted to help other people sell records,' she revealed later, in an interview with *Rolling Stone*. All of that behind-the-scenes knowledge that her teachers had given her had made her feel this sort of role might be more profitable. So she might have become one of the people behind the scenes – with an important role to play but no public recognition. We might have been denied that beautiful voice. Instead, an encounter with an A&R man would lead to Adele herself selling records – and lots of them. It was May 2006. She had left the Brit School and turned eighteen, celebrating with a party in a Brixton pub. She stood up and sang a few songs. In the audience was Nick Huggett, an A&R man for XL Recordings.

At this stage, Adele had written three songs and her friend Lyndon had posted rough recordings of the tracks – 'Hometown Glory', 'Daydreamer' and 'My Same' – on Myspace, the favoured social network of Lily Allen. Huggett remembered when he first heard Adele's tracks. A talent scout had recommended he give a listen to the songs by a teenager from London. At the time, Huggett was in Barcelona with the rap star Dizzee Rascal, who was on tour with the Red Hot Chili Peppers. 'I just heard a really amazing voice and I thought "Wow, there's something special about this girl" and went to investigate her further.' Huggett was almost floored by the strength of her voice, which was clear even on the basic recording. 'I remember it very distinctly because the hairs on the back of my neck stood up,' he recalled. 'It was the voice and emotion that caught my attention; I felt it in a way that you don't very often.'

He was not about to let a talent like that slip through his fingers. He decided to contact Adele directly and kept his fingers crossed that she would be interested in what he had to offer. However, the initial exchanges did not go the way he expected. When she received Huggett's message, Adele assumed it was from 'some internet perv' and completely ignored it. When she received follow-up messages from him, she replied, 'Can you not email me please? I'm busy.' Huggett in turn replied, 'I'm sorry, I just wanted to check: are you signed?' Adele asked him, 'Signed to what?' and he said, 'Have you got a record deal?' A meeting was arranged, but Adele still wasn't convinced that he wanted to sign her as an artist. She thought that what the label really wanted was to employ her as an intern! In the end, Huggett asked fellow London artist Jack Peñate to vouch for him. Adele agreed to meet him and took her friend, Ben Thomas, along for the chat. During an interview with the *Observer*, she acknowledged that Thomas was 'puny' and 'like a dwarf', but she hoped he would provide some sort of physical heft if things turned sinister. Perhaps her choice of bodyguard suggests Adele did not really think she was in any sort of danger, but rather that she felt nervous and overwhelmed by the idea of meeting a record label.

Huggett collected Adele and her friend from the tube station and drove them to the XL Recordings' office. When she realized that the label did indeed want to sign her, she felt 'fucking excited', she said. However, her excitement was complicated by the fact that she was thinking of continuing with her studies. A move to the Liverpool Institute for Performing Arts was on the cards, creating a dilemma for Adele. Should she sign the deal or continue with her studies. 'She was asking me what she should do,' said Huggett, in an interview quoted in the *NME*. 'I said, "I can't tell you what to do." Looking back now, you might say of course she should've gone for music, but at the time, that would've been a hard thing for me to say to an eighteen year old. You don't want to be the person to fuck someone's life up. It was a good lesson for me.'

Adele chose the XL Recordings route. Like her mother before her, she had planned to go to art college at eighteen, only for fate to intervene and take her in a different direction. For Penny, this was motherhood. For Adele, this would be fame. After the ink dried on the deal, Adele quickly became a regular presence in her label's somewhat humble headquarters, but in an incongruous way. 'She would come and hang out at the office because she was a bit bored,' Huggett said. 'One day she came in to stuff envelopes, which looking back, just seems so strange.' She also undertook shift work at the Rough Trade Records shop.

Huggett not only got Adele a record deal, he helped find her a manager. This might be considered not the best way of choosing representation – part of a good manager's appeal is often a degree of distance from the record label, so he can offer independent advice when the artist feels at odd with the label. Yet when Huggett recommended her to Jonathan Dickins, who had founded a company called September

Management, she signed up with the boss. Dickins said that 'from the start it was clear she had this absolutely god-given talent' and 'the best voice I've ever heard in my life'. He wanted to win her over and he did: he made Adele laugh so much when they first met that she had stomach cramps the following day. He also made, she remembered later, a 'great cup of tea'. That, and the fact that Dickins already managed one of her favourite acts, Jamie T, was enough to convince her. Dickins remembered that he 'threw in some ideas' of his own and 'generally it just clicked'. Ultimately, signing Adele was 'one of the most easy, uncomplicated things I've ever done,' he said.

Adele celebrated the record deal surrounded by friends and family at the Duke of Wellington pub in Notting Hill. She felt happy but overwhelmed by the deal that had 'come out of nowhere'. She said she 'got really scared' and had a panic attack when she realized what she had to do next – she had to actually write an album. In other words, she made a career commitment and then freaked out a bit when the enormity of it struck her – a reaction that would show its head a number of times in her career. Every artist needs some inspiration, and for her debut album, as we have seen, Adele found it in the form of a 'rubbish boyfriend'. They dated for several months and he became her most serious boyfriend to date. 'I would have died for him,' she said. Then, she discovered he had been cheating on her. Adele was furious. She stormed into a bar where she knew he was having a drink, berated him and then 'punched him in the face'. The staff quickly ejected her from the venue.

That might have been that, but this episode was going to inspire her first song. Because her (by now ex) boyfriend did not follow her out of the bar to plead for understanding or remonstrate, she found herself alone on Oxford Street in the early hours of the morning. This was where a crucial inspiration struck. 'I got thrown out, and as I was running away, the phrase "chasing pavements" came to me,' she told *Rolling Stone*. 'I sang it into my phone.' She made her way home, and when she arrived back in West Norwood she picked up her guitar and wrote the music for what would become one of her best loved songs: 'Chasing Pavements'.

Curiously, concrete played a part in the inspiration for one of her other early classics. Many people assume that 'Hometown Glory' was written about West Norwood, but Adele has confirmed it was actually conceived in a much more urban location. It is true that Adele wrote the song after her mother tried to persuade her to leave her home suburb of West Norwood in London for university. 'I was about to attend university in Liverpool and I changed my mind,' she said. 'I didn't want to move out of London and leave my friends and family behind.'

Penny tried to convince her daughter to make the move nonetheless. 'My mum said if I wanted my independence, I should go,' Adele told *HITS Daily Double*. 'Because I depend on her so. I love her so much. She's my best friend. I'm such a mommy's girl. She told me, if I stayed in London, ran out of money and couldn't pay the rent, she would always be around to help me. And that's not learning to live on my own or standing on my own two feet. And we had a big argument about it, and I ran upstairs, cried my eyes out, wrote "Hometown Glory", came back down, sang it to her and told her I was staying. And she said: "Alright."' Penny was the first audience for a song that would later be played around the world, with many millions hearing it.

Adele said it took her just ten minutes to compose the song, with its 'four chords pressing one string'. However, the first nugget of inspiration had actually struck her a few years earlier. She was only fourteen but had enjoyed a night of drinking and revelry at a club in Holborn. As she walked down the road afterwards, she was drunkenly staggering along the road, trying to avoid stepping on the cracks in the pavement. This made for quite a sight. 'I was really pissed, wobbling all over the place,' she remembered later in an interview with *Q*. 'This French woman comes up to me and goes "You need help, dah-ling?" And I went "Nah, it's me hometown, luv."'

Another of the lines – about two worlds colliding and people taking different sides – was inspired on a different occasion. 'I went on a march against the Iraq war,' she said of the famous February 2003 demonstration. 'I'm not into politics. I know nothing about them. It was just such a moment, to see all these people come together to stand against something. There were skinhead punks hanging out with rude-boy kids in hoodies … all in one place, marching through the city. I'd never seen anything like it, even in the movies. It was great to be a part of it.'

Overall, Adele told *Blues & Soul*, the song is 'a kind of protest song about cherishing the memories – whether good or bad – of your hometown'. She added that although it is a song about London, she doesn't say the capital city's name, so 'it can be about anywhere'. The dominant themes of her debut album are similarly universal. Anyone who has had their heart broken will find a lot to relate to here. She continues to write as universally as possible. Adele is not interested in in-jokes or niche, 'cool' references. She is interested in authenticity. 'I was very sad when I wrote it,' said Adele of her debut album, 'and I think that genuinely does come through in the music.'

Slowly, the tracks that would form her first album were coming together, and as they were bubbling up, Adele also took to the road. In the early months of 2007 she played some pub venues and then she was the support act for a tour by singer-songwriter Jack Peñate. The two had met in a pub and became very close. 'He's been there before anyone else,' said Adele. So, what were Adele's earliest gigs actually like? The writer Tom Lamont, who would, much later, conduct a landmark interview with Adele for the *Observer* was present at one of her early performances. It was 2007, and the venue was a 'sweaty and densely packed' Scala in King's Cross, London. 'She was an appendage name on the bill, unknown – performing a couple of songs after a rapper called Lethal Bizzle,' he remembered. He also recalled that the audience were quite bored by the hip-hop performer's set. 'Then Adele walked on stage with an acoustic guitar and a beer and tamed the belligerent room in an instant,' he wrote in the *Observer*. Her stage presence was remarked upon by many of those who saw her earliest concerts.

Progress was happening on all fronts but the simple truth is that without the heartache from the mystery ex, the album would have come together much more slowly and might have never been completed. Having signed the record deal in September 2006, by February 2007 she had only written four songs. 'I was overwhelmed by the deal because it came out of nowhere,' she said. 'Then I met and broke up with my ex and the songs just poured out.' With the material gushing out, what she needed was wider exposure and she got it when she was invited onto the show she had watched as a child: *Later ... with Jools Holland*. It was, and is, a rarity for acts to be invited on before they have made a single release. 'When we fall for somebody, we have to have them,' the show's producer, Alison Howe, told the *Guardian*. 'She's a classic. She doesn't fit anywhere; she just has a great voice.' Adele remembered how nervous she was. Penny came to see her backstage and Adele couldn't even speak, she was so anxious. 'I think she was worried I was gonna fall off my chair or faint or just fuck it up somehow,' said Adele. Note again how her nerves kicked in when the reality of the moment struck her.

'They usually put you in the middle of the room, but for some reason they put me at the end, right in front of the audience,' she said. Björk was to her left and on her right was Sir Paul McCartney. She sat on her stool, strummed her guitar and sang 'Daydreamer'. Howe remembered Adele's performance as 'simple, and almost naïve', and one that was actually enhanced by Adele's nerves. She was able to work on her nerves as she played a series of live shows in the coming months, including performances at festivals in Brighton and Glastonbury. These slots brought back memories of the open-air events she had been to as a child in Finsbury Park and Glastonbury.

Ahead of the album *19*'s launch, came the release of Adele's first single: 'Hometown Glory'. On 22 October 2007, record shop owners added her first release to their shelves. At this stage, she was an unknown, and it felt as if the shops were giving her a leg-up. But, within a matter of years the record shop industry would consider Adele an economic powerhouse whose mammoth sales were propping up their sector and offering it a future, at a time when a myriad of factors threatened their very existence. The B-side of the single was 'Fool That I Am' by Adele's idol, Etta James – that fateful trip to HMV was raising its head. In the wake of the single's release, Adele gained more media attention. She was on *Friday Night with Jonathan Ross*, where she sang 'Chasing Pavements', and then she sang on a BBC Radio 2 gig in Shepherd's Bush, west London. The *Guardian* ran a piece on Adele headlined: 'Watch out Amy Winehouse!'

Her level of public recognition soared again when she won the first ever Critics' Choice Award (now the Rising Star Award) at the 2008 annual BRIT Awards celebration of music. While the winners of most awards are announced on the night of the ceremony, for this inaugural award the panel decided to announce it two months beforehand. This brought a lot of attention to the award and a lot of attention to Adele – not all of it favourable. She told *The Times* the honour was 'really weird'. Speaking of the recognition and success she was already enjoying, she added: 'I just hope it doesn't peak too soon. It's encouraging that everything's going so well, but obviously I haven't actually released the [album] yet, so it's all a bit ridiculous.'

A second single was released before the album emerged. 'Chasing Pavements' was released in January 2008. Again, a cover was chosen for the B-side. This time Sam Cooke's 'That's It – I Quit – I'm Movin' On'. With her media profile much higher than when her debut single came out, this time she reached Number Two in the UK charts. An endorsement from Kanye West didn't hurt, either. During a promotional interview for the single's release, she was asked to define her sound. 'I'd call it heartbroken soul – pathetic love songs about being pathetic!' she said. 'I was listening back to my album the other day, and I just thought "Oh my god, I'm so pathetic when it comes to boys!"'

Meanwhile, work was going ahead on her album. The collection was recorded and mixed between April and October 2007, produced by Jim Abbiss, Mark Ronson and Eg White. Adele credited Abbiss with 'capturing the moments', Ronson for 'bringing the tune to life' and White for letting her 'moan about love productively'. It was named after the age she was when she was writing it, establishing a titular formula she has stuck with until this day. This is not a decision she has come to lightly, because Adele has strong opinions on many things, including album titles. She likes keeping them simple and memorable. 'The best ones for me are *Debut* by Björk and Lauryn Hill's *Miseducation*. They're ones that everyone just knows, that don't make you think too much and are just quite obvious,' she said.

In any case, there was for her no better way to represent where – or when – the album sprang from. 'To me this album does very much represent my age,' she told *Blues & Soul*. 'I was only nineteen years old when I was writing it, and I just kind of remember becoming a bit of a woman during that time. And I think that is definitely documented in the songs. When I was signed at eighteen, I only had three songs to my name. But yet, literally within a month of turning nineteen, a load more just suddenly came out of me.'

She had split up with her first proper boyfriend, and this is what caused that sudden eruption. 'It took a lot from me to write the album,' she told *Mic* magazine. 'Instead of going off and asking people to write songs for me, I kind of put my head down and tried my hardest to admit things to myself and to put it into songs. It's a break-up record from the very bottom of my soul, as cheesy as that sounds.' She then explained how the songs were composed. 'That album genuinely did just come together very naturally and very organically,' she said. 'I will sit in my room on my own for ages. I can't be around anyone. And I'll write. That's how that atmosphere gets created.'

Adele had strict standards even back then, and one of them was that she didn't want to be lazy, particularly when it came to the words. 'I hate – I'm actually offended by – literal easy lyrics that have no thought behind them and are purely written because they rhyme. I had no specific plans for my album,' she told *Blues & Soul*. 'In fact, I still don't know exactly what kind of artist I want to be!' Listeners could find out what kind of artist they thought she was as they listened to *19*.

'Daydreamer' is a mellow and pure start to the album. In this bittersweet track, she dreams of her perfect man and lists his wonderful qualities, in absolutely yearning language and vocals. However, she ultimately confesses, what she is describing is only what she is hoping for. The song blends modern urban sass with a twist of Nina Simone. The track itself was influenced by a boy she was 'in proper love with', Adele explained on her official website. Their relationship went awry when she discovered he was bisexual. While having no quarrel with bisexuality, Adele simply felt that her 'jealous' side would not be able to withstand 'having to fight off the boys as well'. When he kissed one of her friends, that was the final straw. 'I was, like: "Get lost!"' She told him: 'We're not even going out yet and you've cheated on me already!'

She wrote the song while she was suffering from a slipped disc. It was, therefore, composed as she lay on her back with her guitar pointing at the ceiling. She was also under the weather with flu at the time, so this song emerged from a feverish place. Perhaps its wistful tone was aided by her yearning for convalescence? The high temperatures of flu can conjure a hallucinogenic and surreal atmosphere, in which what is happening in your head can blur with what is happening in reality. In any case, with its basic and beautiful production, 'Daydreamer' is, indeed, very dreamy to listen to.

'Best for Last', the second song on *19*, arrives with some more instrumentation. The sad lyrics of unrequited love are somewhat belied by the upbeat music, which is driven by funky bass, played by Adele herself. The soulful backing vocals from The Life Gospel Choir, who sing while Adele tells the subject of the song that he is merely a 'temporary fix', are a nice touch on this, one of Adele's most underrated tracks. This jazzily toned tune features a notably husky emotion from Adele that belied her teenage years. The sassy, urban pronunciation of the vocals of her early years is most clear here. The *Observer* described 'Best for Last' as 'a schoolgirl on the top deck of a bus nonchalantly channelling Aretha [Franklin]', which does the trick well.

The third song, 'Chasing Pavements', was, said Adele, a 'big Burt Bacharach-tinged and almost middle-of-the-road' track. After two gentler songs opened the album with not much more than a whisper, here is where *19* begins to bang. This is a song that answered her wanting for a 'radio song' and 'big commercial tune'. This old-school soul track sees the power of her voice emerge, as it guides the brassy, soaring chorus of this sophisticated song. In quality, it is anything but middle-of-the-road. Adele has said she is 'very proud' of 'Chasing Pavements'. She should be.

NME called it a 'booming shout-out from the middle of the yellow brick road to fame ... literally drenched with ... showgirl chutzpah'. Paul Weller, who would join her for a television performance of the track, said it was the Adele song he wishes he had written. It would be nominated for three GRAMMY Awards and become her signature song for the early years of her career, loved by audiences around the world. As for Adele, she said that she found the way people have 'connected' with 'Chasing Pavements' is 'amazing'.

Yet, for many listeners, 'Chasing Pavements' is not the album's highlight. Mark Ronson was at the controls for the song that many favour – the sassy 'Cold Shoulder'. This funky and fresh song is one of *19*'s most danceable songs and takes the album in a different direction. Its groovy guitar and rolling drums are enough to get your hips moving. It's psychedelic, Beatles-style middle eight only adds to the wonder. The anger of the song is one that foreshadows the more defiant notes of her later album, *21*. Long forgotten is the sweeter, gentler Adele of 'Daydreamer'. The lyric about 'words made of knives' is probably *19*'s most edgy moment.

'When I first played the song "Cold Shoulder" to XL it had no beats,' remembered Adele. 'It was just vocals and keyboards. But, while they really liked it and thought it was charming, I was, like, "No, you're wrong! Right now my album lacks rhythm! We need something fast on it!"' She said she wanted Ronson brought in for the song, but when they eventually met she was, she remembered, 'pissed off my face, smoking cigarettes and watching Jerry Springer.' It was not an auspicious start but it led to a successful collaboration and one of the album's most popular songs. *NME* declared it the highlight of *19*, thanks to its 'flickering, panoramic production' and 'totemic timbre'.

We are back to Adele and her guitar for 'Crazy for You'. This track, which beautifully evokes the 1950s, has been described as coming from a series of different genres, from jazz and country to folk and blues. What is clear is that the popular musical themes of infatuation and unrequited love have rarely been rendered as cutely as they are here. Even within the canon of Adele tracks that are based on those themes, this one stands out from the pack. The listener ends up yearning for Adele to find happiness with the subject of the song as she delivers this track, which evokes memories of Patsy Cline.

Next up comes 'Melt My Heart to Stone'. Despite its paradoxical title, this is a track that hits the listener directly in the heart. It features one of Adele's most emotional and hard-hitting vocals. She said she wrote it when she was still raw from her break-up. It is one of the tracks from *19* that could have sat most neatly on her later albums. You can easily imagine it on *25* or *30*, in particular. It is a show-stopping vocal, and this helps lift what would otherwise be a lesser track to greater heights. 'I just love singing it,' she said in an interview quoted in the biography *Adele* by Katherine Krohn. 'When I wrote it, I was crying.' However, she has also stated that the song would be difficult for her to sing live without breaking down. Listen closely and you might detect the odd crack and wobble even in the studio version. Adele is so fond of this song that when she set up her first company, she named it Melting Stone Ltd.

The yo-yo effect between bigger and smaller songs continues as we scale down for 'First Love'. One of 19's less remarkable tracks, it is nevertheless a thing of beauty, confirming that an average Adele song outclasses great songs by other artists. The scant celesta and triangle accompaniment has a lullaby quality to it. Here, she is asking her lover to forgive her because she needs to get away from him. She begs him not to get so close that he makes her doubt herself and vows that she needs a kiss from someone new. However, the narrative is overshadowed by her resigned tone. The song, which lacks a conventional chorus, has been described as having a monologue quality. She plays celesta on the album version of the song.

As we have seen, early in her career Adele was often compared to Amy Winehouse. This was in some ways an overblown comparison to make, but if there is a crossover musically, it is seen clearly in 'Right as Rain'. In a way, it is a meta expression of Adele's material to date: the upside of things going wrong. For here is a celebration of when things go wrong. Introducing the song live on stage, she has said it is an attempt to put a positive feeling on things 'when you're feeling shit'. To a rhythm and blues track, fused with sixties soul and a hint of Motown, she does indeed explore the upside of heartbreak. This song has a large army of songwriters: those credited include Leon Michels, Jeff Silverman, Nick Movshon and Clay Holley. On the comparisons with Winehouse, Adele was gracious. 'I love Amy Winehouse and I love her music as well,' she said. 'So I have no problem being compared to her. At least I like her. If it was someone like Joss Stone, I would be very unhappy.'

Then comes a cover, of the Bob Dylan song 'Make You Feel My Love'. This song has been widely covered by other artists, including Billy Joel, Neil Diamond, Ronan Keating and Bryan Ferry. It takes some audacity to cover the great Dylan, and a lot of attempts have proven misguided. Many critics, including the music authority Paul Gambaccini, consider Adele's version the greatest take on it of all, which is immense praise. The *Observer* said that Adele 'summons a passion that its croaking author could only envy'.

Jonathan Dickins played Dylan's version to Adele and suggested she cover it, seemingly in a bid to add another radio-friendly track to the 19 collection. At first, Adele was not sure. She believes that a song has an emotional bond to its writer which it is unwise to attempt to replicate. However, she changed her mind. 'The song is so convincing,' she said, adding that it 'just kind of sums up that sour point in my life I've been trying to get out of my system and write into songs'.

Again, there would prove to be a Winehouse connection here. In 2011, two weeks after the tragedy-hit singer died, Adele was performing in Vancouver, Canada. She announced that she was dedicating the song that night to Amy. This dedication became a tradition at future concerts. Fans would hold up their phones with their lights on after Adele asked them to, 'so that Amy can see them from upstairs'.

Adele's version of the song has proven to have a long life commercially. It has featured on the soundtracks of various popular UK TV shows, including *Hollyoaks*, *Eastenders* and *Waterloo Road*, prompting spikes in sales. Rebecca Ferguson sang Adele's version on *The X Factor*, giving it another lift. It has also featured on *Strictly Come Dancing*, *Britain's Got Talent* and the *Comic Relief* TV show, and has become one of the longest-running singles in the UK singles chart. For all its potency and splendour, there is a mild emotional disconnect in her delivery of the poignant vocals. Perhaps, ultimately, Adele's emotional connection with songs is that bit stronger when she has written the lyrics herself, unlike the Nina Simones of this world.

'My Same' is Adele at her sassiest, complete with a glorious 'pffft'. This fusion of jazz and rockabilly sees Adele sing about her friendship with her friend Laura Dockrill. Although the two are opposites, they get along, she says. Adele declined to sing the song live for a while because she and Laura had fallen out – 'probably over something stupid'. Not everyone quite believes that she has forgotten what caused them to row. However, they were later reunited by the singer Jessie Ware, who had been writing with Dockrill. The *Guardian* said 'My Same' was a 'finger-popping strut that is really charming, the vocal performance assured enough to make you disregard the lyrics, which occasionally betray its author's youth'. It certainly has attitude aplenty. In September 2011, before she performed the song in the

Royal Albert Hall, Adele asked Laura to stand up. Her friend was dressed in red, white and blue, prompting Adele to comment: 'I'm sure you can tell how different we are: she wears bright colours, I wear black. But she's the love of my life.' Friendship with Adele looks like it is rarely a boring experience.

If you were to read the lyrics to 'Tired' you would imagine a far less jaunty affair than it is. The biggest surprise in this cheeky track, which at times is reminiscent of both Lily Allen and Amy Winehouse, is the middle eight. The strings offer this section a Coldplay edge. The Adele of the lyrics may be tired of putting so much into a relationship and not getting 'nuffin' back', but this song has plenty of energy. It is comparatively easy-going, which sets up an even greater change of pace for the gravitas of the album's closer.

The album concludes with 'Hometown Glory'. For many listeners this meant the best was left until last, a trick she repeated on her next album. Adele is very particular about track sequencing on albums and considers this an art form in itself. Some artists have concluded that in this digital age, when people often just download two or three tracks, or compile their own playlists, track sequencing is not as important as it was in the days when people bought a vinyl record and sat patiently listening to the songs in the sequence the artist put them in. Adele is different, she still believes sequencing is important and is uncomfortable with the pick-and-mix atmosphere of the streaming era. So it seems no coincidence that she has, more than once, put the biggest and boldest track of the album at the end.

The album in its entirety was bold: in her teenage debut, Adele had included a range of styles, from blues to folk rock, indie pop, and jazz influences in the forty-three minutes and forty-one seconds of *19*. There was also soul, although Adele insists that she 'never at any stage thought, "Ooh, I'm going to be a white soul girl!"' The themes of heartbreak, love, community and nostalgia are all beautifully rendered. As quoted earlier, she told *Blues & Soul* that 'I just kinda remember becoming a bit of a woman during that time, and I think that is definitely documented in the songs.'

The album was released on 28 January 2008 and reached Number One in the UK charts. Adele was thrilled, naturally. 'Going to Number One was the most amazing thing that has happened or will ever happen,' she said. It is true that more amazing things would happen for Adele in subsequent years, but many artists say that their first big chart success remains their favourite, however much more glory they enjoy.

Then it was time for Adele to await the critical verdicts of the reviewers. She and her music had enjoyed more pre-release hype than most debut artists receive. The critics can sometimes be annoyed by such favourable headlines and then sharpen their pencils all the more when it comes to offering their verdict. Adele would indeed receive a few grudging notices but there was also plentiful praise for *19*.

One of the most glowing reviews came in the *Observer*, which had previously tipped her as 'one to watch'. Caspar Llewellyn Smith slathered five stars onto *19* and declared Adele the greatest female vocalist of 2008. He said the 'perfectly paced record' was an 'outstanding debut'. He purred that there is an 'artistically focused stillness at the centre of so many of these bruising love songs'. Referring to her inspirations and geographical location, he invites readers to regard Adele as 'Dusty or Aretha, albeit of SW2'. Pete Paphides of *The Times* wrote that after hearing her singing of heartache, 'you feel like bringing her a mug of warm sweet milk and a saucer of Hobnobs, before trying to convince her that no man is worth this sort of heartache'. He added, 'She may well agree. But would she believe it if you told her that no album is worth this sort of heartache? Probably not. And, when you hear *19*, neither will you.'

Chuck Taylor said in *Billboard* magazine that Adele 'truly has potential to become among the most respected and inspiring international artists of her generation'. Chris Long, of BBC Music, said 'her melodies exude warmth, her singing is occasionally stunning and … she has tracks that make Lily Allen and Kate Nash sound every bit as ordinary as they are'. A writer for the Digital Spy website felt that Adele was 'alternately sassy, vulnerable, needy, apathetic and … even political'.

However, *NME* was less upbeat. Noting the comparisons between Adele and Winehouse, Priya Elan wrote, 'Yes, she's the charismatic London lass done good. Yes, she possesses the oak-aged voice that belies her Botticelli face, but … really?' Elan awarded the album just five stars out of ten and added that 'there's precious little on the album that prevents it from collapsing under the weight of its own expectation'.

Uncut magazine was also cynical, concluding that although Adele 'can certainly sing', the album 'reeks of some

A&R trendhound making it his/her biz to sign The New Amy and not resting till s/he's found the right chick from south London to fit the bill'. Andy Gill of the *Independent* said the album was only 'passably decent' but 'could have been so much more by being so much less anticipated'. The *Guardian*'s Dorian Lynskey was also distinctly unimpressed. 'There is scant emotional heft behind Adele's prodigiously rich voice,' he wrote, and 'little bite to her songwriting'. Awarding the album just two stars out of five, he complained that 'too many self-conscious ballads underline the difference between soul, which can shake you into feeling something new, and MOR, which merely soothes and affirms'.

SPIN magazine's Barry Walters felt there was a mix of 'rough and smooth' in the album's 'glut of mawkish breakup ballads', some of which he felt were 'blandly clunky'. He gave the album two and a half stars. *Rolling Stone*, meanwhile, offered three out of five. The least positive review came on the Sputnikmusic website, which said the collection was 'music for fat, pubescent girls'.

Adele told the *Guardian* she read reviews at the start of her career but then largely avoided them. That said, she turned her back on them with a healthy sense of self-awareness. 'I read them at the beginning,' she said. 'But then there were a few nasty ones and I thought: I'm not going to bother with them anymore. I don't mind them that much, though. It's normal, innit? I go on YouTube and leave nasty things on there. If I was a really nice person and was, like, "Let's just live in harmony," I'd be upset. But I can be a bitch as well.' This grounded view of reviews is a rarity among artists, many of whom complain bitterly if their work is badly received.

There was a question mark over what motivated some of the feedback, however. Some have speculated that those who criticized *19* were doing so as part of a backlash against acts who had been discovered on Myspace. While there was much excitement over the fact that Lily Allen and Arctic Monkeys found fame and success through that route, eventually some in the music journalism sector took against the trend. There was also, perhaps, an unease and suspicion in some corners that Adele had risen to prominence so quickly. Some simply opposed the fact that she had been awarded a BRIT gong so young. In February 2008, the *Independent* wrote that 'the instant success that the hype surrounding Adele brings could work to her disadvantage', adding, 'Unlike those artists who have built up success more slowly and established a loyal following over the years, Adele has only a relatively newly acquired fanbase ... will she stay at the top?'

As she continued to enjoy a high profile very early in her career, she was booked to appear on the irreverent pop TV panel show *Never Mind the Buzzcocks* in 2008. In many ways, she fitted the bill perfectly for the show, which likes to puncture the egos of pampered pop stars. The show's cheeky host, Simon Amstell, introduced her, saying, 'She normally spends her time chasing pavements. Well, pavements can take a night off because tonight she's chasing points!'

So far, so good. However, it was not long before Amstell was trying to goad Adele into being rude about other female pop stars. 'Do you want to know why I like you?' he asked. 'Because you're down to earth, you're likeable, you're like the perfect human being. You're real, you tell it like it is, and you're honest.' Adele is no fool, so she knew something more was coming. 'Yes?' she said, knowingly. Amstell continued, 'So tell us who you hate most out of Lily Allen, Kate Nash and Duffy.' As she giggled, Amstell added: 'Tell us why you hate Duffy so much.'

Adele was not about to get drawn into that. 'No, I don't hate Duffy,' she said. 'But I'm Welsh as well and I wish people would know that, because my nanna gets quite upset. No one recognizes that I'm Welsh. But she is full Welsh, but then she's north Welsh.' Amstell was not about to be thrown off the scent. 'Also, in interviews you feel that Duffy comes across as a bit fake, right?' he said. She replied: 'Why are you doing this?' Amstell then asked if she thought Duffy was a 'lying bitch'. She was game enough to know she had to throw him a scrap, so, later in the show, she said of Lindsay Lohan: 'I think she's lovely, but she's not an actress'. She said later that she preferred radio slots to television appearances, because the latter are 'boring' backstage. She complained that 'everyone's an a***ehole' in the TV world and she found the experience ruined her own enjoyment of television as a viewer.

There was a more than a hint of a backlash against Adele at the 2008 BRITs ceremony, when a fellow award-winner threw some shade her way. It had all started so well. Her hero Will Young introduced Adele, saying that the fact her album was at Number One vindicated the decision to give her the Critics' Choice Award. He then asked for a round of applause for the 'gorgeous' Adele. Clearly nervous, she said, 'I am not going to talk for too long because I think speeches are really boring, but I would really like to thank some people.' She also complained that her heart was beating 'so fast' before handing out some praise for her team, including the BRIT School and her 'beautiful mum'.

So far so good, but her performance of 'God Put a Smile Upon Your Face' was not a classic, and then Arctic Monkeys teased her when they stepped up to accept their award for Best British Group. 'We all went to the BRIT School,' said lead singer Alex Turner. 'We remember you all. After we graduated, we formed the Monkeys and we've had a fantastic time since.' The BRIT School principal played the matter down when he said it was 'a bit of fluff', but Adele was less forgiving. 'Fucking idiots,' she said. 'Think they're working class. Their bloody mums are art teachers, aren't they?'

Her public brashness masked a private vulnerability. She met Robbie Williams shortly after the awards show and told him that she felt 'uncomfortable' about the prize. 'I was getting criticized for the first time, with people saying I only won because I'd been to the BRIT School,' she told the *Daily Mail*. 'They thought I'd been manufactured … but I'd paid my dues with some tough gigs.' She said Williams was very supportive. 'He told me the prize was just a leg-up: it had put me in a position where people would listen,' she said. 'That helped.'

Later, she was able to respond to the episode with more confidence and humour, as she addressed the suggestion that the award was created purely to create hype around her. 'I don't think it was invented for me, that would be really, really funny if it was, wouldn't it? I mean: "Oh my gosh!"' she said. 'But yeah, you know, I think it's a really good award. The impression I got from the award, and why they announced it in December, was to bring the spotlight on the person that won it. I'm getting a lot of coverage at the moment so it's very successful in what it set out to do. So I think they should have it every year.'

She was asked if she had considered, even for a moment, rejecting it. 'No, I'm an opportunist!' she said. ''Course I'm not going to turn it down! I've always wanted one, as well. You know, the hype and all that, there's not a lot I can do about it. I'm getting a bit sick of seeing myself in stuff, but I haven't actually done many interviews. It's just people writing about it. It happens, you know!'

It does, but the nominations would keep on coming: *19* attracted a Mercury Prize nomination for best album of the year. Also up for the prize were acts including Elbow, Rachel Unthank & The Winterset, British Sea Power, and Radiohead. The winner was Elbow, with *The Seldom Seen Kid*. But Adele had been excited to be in the running for such an honour and among such accomplished acts.

As for the ex who inspired *19*, she said felt 'grateful' to him. 'I got a multi-platinum album out of it and he still works at a phone shop,' she said. She told the *Sun* newspaper that he tried to convince her to cut him in on the royalties for *19*. 'For about a week he was calling and was deadly serious about it,' she said. 'He really thought he'd had some input into the creative process by being a prick.' Over the years, the financial takings from *19* have been huge. It was a Number One in the UK and it has become a global success, also reaching Number One in Netherlands, and hitting the Top Ten in twelve countries including Australia, Brazil and the United States. The album has gone on to be certified eight times platinum by BPI (the British record labels association) with sales of over 2.4 million, and has been certified three times platinum in the US by RIAA, the Recording Industry Association of America, having sold over 3 million copies there. As of 2022, the album had sold over 6.5 million copies worldwide, as sales continue to spike with the release of subsequent Adele albums.

19 attracted four GRAMMY Award nominations: Best New Artist for Adele, and Record of the Year, Song of the Year and Best Female Pop Vocal Performance for 'Chasing Pavements'. She won an Urban Music Award for Best Jazz Act and a *Q* Awards nomination in the category of Breakthrough Act, as well as a Music of Black Origin nomination in the category of Best UK Female. If Adele had hung up her musical ambitions after the release of *19*, she would still stand in the history books. However, there was no chance of that as she felt she was still searching for her musical identity.

All the same, if that ex had convinced Adele to cut him in to the royalties for *19*, he would have attracted a tidy sum. She gave his cheeky request short shrift, telling him that after the misery he had inflicted upon her she deserved to keep all the riches that her debut album had won her. However, he remains an influential figure in modern music history. Few people can say they have inspired an album that went on to sell millions of copies around the world. He told Adele that he 'loves' the album, adding: 'It's about me.' Adele corrected him, saying: 'It's about heartbreak, you fool!'

And yet there were much bigger, and happier, times ahead for Adele. In 2021, she was asked what she wishes she had told herself when she was nineteen. 'I would've been a baby, wouldn't I?' she replied, adding that she would have told herself 'to enjoy it all' because 'I don't think I had enjoyed most of it so far'. She added: 'I wish I'd known to go a little bit deeper in myself, for myself, so that I could enjoy it all.'

The truth was already clear: for all the pleasure Adele derived from being a professional singer, there were aspects of the experience that she found hard to take. Her first response was to try and dig deeper into the musical experience itself. The journey to that depth would continue with her second album, which would blow the world away and establish Adele as such an iconic talent that those sneering, doubting voices would be silenced, as her voice became the soundtrack to millions of lives, a healing force for the broken-hearted.

CHAPTER THREE

COMING OF AGE

I n a century when many pop acts are more focused on their images than their material, musical laziness has grown. Given the success of her debut album and her still relatively tender years as she begun work on her follow-up album, it might have crossed Adele's mind to simply produce a second *19*. However, she is such a restless artist that this was never going to be the direction she chose. In fact, she wanted to go bigger and brassier. In doing so, she hoped, she would find who she was. 'I feel a lot bolder now in terms of what the songs are about so I wanted a bit of oomph behind them,' said Adele of her second album. She said she was also in search of a 'body of work' with an 'Adele sound'. As well as seeking to catch her sound, Adele's second album would chart the emotional journey she was going on when she wrote it, entrenching her tradition of creating albums in the style of personal journals. 'I was really angry,' she said of the time. 'Then I was bitter. Then I was really lonely, and then I was devastated. It was in that order – the record.'

Between her first and second albums, said Adele, she had what she called an 'early life crisis' which sent her 'a bit doolally'. She was struggling because of the success and fame that 19 had brought her. As we shall see, Adele has never seemingly fully adjusted to the pressures of fame. Many of the controversies that have hit her can be understood by this discomfort she feels from success and public recognition – and felt from the very first time she tasted fame.

'I try not to moan about it,' she told the *Observer* later of her first crisis. 'But I just wasn't prepared for my success at all and I went a bit doolally for a while. I needed some time off and I wasn't really getting it, so I just tried to kind of make up excuses to be given a break.' For a girl who only recently had been sleeping in and missing classes at school, and then drinking cider in the park with her friends, life was suddenly very different. She was told where she had to be and when. A team would make sure she was ready on time, and that 'time' often involved early starts and long journeys. Then there was the pressure that she felt as a solo artist whose appeal was so based on the precision of her voice. Unlike a reluctant band member who can hide in the shadows when they are not 'feeling it', Adele had to be there and be on form every time. Whether it was singing live on stage or facing unpredictable questions from a stranger who just happened to be a journalist, she felt exposed and had, to say the least, mixed feelings about this.

One day, she had a blazing row with the paparazzi when she discovered them waiting outside her home. She had always loathed these sorts of predatory photographers and on that day she left them in no doubt of her feelings. Embarrassingly, she then realized they were not there for a snap of her but of the supermodel Elle Macpherson. Adele hadn't realized she had a model living next door.

She became frustrated that the demands of her new career took her away from her friends. When they phoned and asked if she wanted to meet up she would be too busy or overseas. She got 'annoyed' by this and so she drew a line in the sand. She told her record company and management team that she needed time off. 'So for three months I went to the pub, barbecues, saw my cousins.'

She told the digital magazine *Nylon* that 'we refer to that period as my E.L.C., my Early Life Crisis'. She admitted that she was 'drinking far too much'. In a separate interview, she said that she was 'really unhappy at home' because 'there were a lot of family issues going on'. She said her excessive alcohol consumption was 'the basis of my relationship with this boy'. That 'boy' was ten years older than Adele and, by all accounts, quite the culture vulture. It is said that he introduced her to novels, smart films, history and curious food. He loved a drink, too. 'We had everything – on every level we were totally right,' she said. 'We'd finish each other's sentences, and he could just pick up how I was feeling by the look in my eye, down to a *T*, and we loved the same things, and hated the same things, and we were brave when the other was weak.'

This was the man who would influence 21. His identity is not known, and yet he is the influential spark behind one of the twenty-first century's most successful albums.

Adele actually set out wanting to produce an album quite different in tone from that of her first. Looking back over *19*, she had concluded that it had not reflected her character, which she sees as 'fun, cheeky, loud and sarcastic'. Charting her emotions of the moment, discovering and rendering the 'Adele sound' and putting her true personality across – it was quite an order paper she had set herself.

Following a month off after the end of a tour, Adele started work on what would become *21*. The first part of the process was to spend several weeks at home, listening to all the artists and albums that had influenced her. Or 'swimming in music', as she put it. Alongside her long-standing trusty faves, such as Tom Waits, Alanis Morissette, Mary J. Blige and Sinéad O'Connor, she also listened to country acts she was unfamiliar with, such as Johnny Cash, the Carter Family and Dolly Parton. It was quite a swim.

Then she got to work, spending time on the album between the spring of 2009 and the autumn of 2010. The songs were written on either side of the Atlantic – in Los Angeles and London. There were rumours that the new album would be a fully fledged country collection, but Adele scotched these. 'I haven't made a country record,' she told the BBC in January 2011. She said she wanted to think that the 'words, feelings and emotions' of the genre had 'rubbed off' on her. 'My accent doesn't suit a country song,' she added, because she lacked 'that twang'.

Nevertheless, she wanted to zoom in on the strong storytelling of country songs, she added. 'Contemporary records can take three minutes to get to the point,' she said, 'and sometimes you don't know what a song is about even when it's finished.' Whereas, in country, 'in the first twenty seconds you know exactly what is going on'. She also took an interest in rockabilly, particularly the sound of Wanda Jackson. Mumford & Sons were another influence; Adele said their material 'literally goes into my chest and beats me up, and makes me completely fearless'.

A key new feature for the album was a loosening of control by Adele, according to her account, at least. 'My first record is about eighty per cent me on my own, this one is about sixty per cent.' She liked this, because, she said, she finds she is 'more forgiving' of herself the more she works with other people. In this regard she particularly lauded Rick Rubin, who she said helped her ease into the process. Every bit the Taurean, she told the *Daily Mail*: 'I'm a control freak and I don't like spontaneity. But he made me go with my instincts and loosen up as I was singing.'

The relationship that would inspire the backbone of the material on 21 had been a big stepping stone in Adele's life. 'It was the biggest deal in my entire life to date … He made me totally hungry … He was older, he was successful in his own right, whereas my boyfriends before were my age and not really doing much,' she told MTV about the relationship. 'He got me interested in film and literature and food and wine and travelling and politics and history, and those were things I was never, ever interested in. I was interested in going clubbing and getting drunk.' Like many older boyfriends, her partner had encouraged her to change. Ultimately, the relationship hit the rocks.

The world was fascinated to hear what the album that emerged from this relationship and its heartbreaking end would sound like. Adele has described the opening track, 'Rolling in the Deep', as a 'dark, bluesy, gospel disco tune'. As is often the case with her, she has also offered a ruder description, saying the song is the equivalent of 'word-vomiting'. However, this is a song that is a world away from anything on *19*, signalling from the start of the new album that it was just that – new. It was written the morning after she had broken up with her 'soul mate'. She arrived at the studio to work with Paul Epworth and, when he learned of her breakup, Epworth encouraged her to vent. Adele was more than capable of that. 'I'm such a fucking drama queen,' she has said. 'I was so angry!' It took just two days to finish fashioning that rage into a song – they ended up using the first take because later versions couldn't capture as much rage.

The composition and recording of 'Rolling in the Deep' proved to be a visceral experience for Adele. 'I guess it's my equivalent of saying things in the heat of the moment and word-vomiting,' she told Digital Spy. 'It takes a lot of shit to get me a bit upset and crazy, so when I get angry in my heart, I can really feel my blood flowing around my body.' Her aims here were simple: firstly, Adele wanted people who listened to the song to think 'Shit, it sounds like she is going to kill him.' However, she added, she also hoped that the song would reflect another side of her. 'I'm really sarcastic, really cheeky, I'm always trying to crack a joke and make people laugh,' she said. 'I think "Rolling in the Deep" is more relevant to that.'

Again, her mission statement for her second album in sum was encapsulated in 'Rolling in the Deep'. She had noticed that 'people always think I'm a serious person, especially off the back of *19* because it's quite a moody record'. She wanted her humour to come across in her new music. Her other aim was to make music that people could dance to. 'When I go and see a live show, it's all ballads, towards the end I get really itchy legs,' Adele told the Idolator music blog. 'I thought I should throw in a couple of upbeat ones so they can kind of work their legs a little bit.' 'Cold Shoulder' was one of the few songs up to that point in her career that could be danced to. 'Rolling in the Deep' was the first track to try and add to that toe-tapping tally.

Adele also wanted to position herself as the victor rather than the villain. She has gathered quite a reputation as a sobbing mess, but her fans are aware that in many of her songs she is sassy and imperious. As she told *SPIN* magazine: 'It's me saying "get the fuck out of my house", instead of me begging him to come back.' She rendered this so well. The *Guardian* said of 'Rolling in the Deep' that 'she hooted, she hollered; she came mob-handed with a host of avenging backing dopplegangers', while the *Sun* praised the 'epic, foot-stomper of a pop anthem with thumping piano and vocal you would expect of a veteran of twenty years on the road'.

Adele called her collaboration with Epworth 'a match made in heaven' and gushed that 'he really brought my voice out of me'. As for Paul, he remembers well how they put this song to bed. As he told *The New York Times*: 'She had had her heart broken, and she was in pieces, and you can really hear that, her anger and her sadness. Sometimes I just don't think you can recreate that or fake it.' It is almost as if she is daring her ex to do her more wrong in this magnificent track. She was so pleased with the track and its title, Adele almost named the album 'Rolling in the Deep', which would have nipped in the bud her tradition of naming albums after her age. It is a great album opener, but the song was originally going to be placed as the sixth track on the album rather than the first.

Track two is 'Rumour Has It' – and here, too, there are plenty of balls compared with anything on *19*. It was written in the US with American songwriter and producer Ryan Tedder, who Adele has described as a 'hit factory'. Again, the process was quick – it took just one day to write and one day to record. 'You can really tell when you hear a Ryan Tedder song,' said Adele, 'which I liked, but I wanted something that would surprise everyone. So we came up with this sort of bluesy, pop, stomping song' with 'dirty guitar'. Adele has a habit of playing down her greatest tracks with a shrug and a sidetrack, as is seen here. She said 'Rumour Has It' is 'not to be taken seriously ... I was fucking hung-over as well, the last thing I wanted to do was try and be emotional.' She added: 'It's basically me just taking the piss.' Many an artist would love to be able to basically take the piss with such genius.

Speaking to a radio interviewer in Canada, she explained the background of the song. 'It's about this boy I met in the summer. I don't trust people very easily. Nothing really happened – we went out on a few dates. And he tried to sell his story to the fucking *Sun* newspaper!' Broadening on the theme of rumours, Adele remembered how once she became famous, her friends would hear gossip about her. This was weird enough, but what Adele found even harder was that her pals would actually believe so much of what they heard. One day, when she came back from the US: 'My friends would be like "I heard this thing in blah blah ... I hope you're not seeing him because I hear he fucked her ... and I heard you're with him ..." It's about my own friends believing stuff that they hear.'

One reviewer said that 'Rumour Has It' was 'Motown on steroids' while another critic felt it was 'a swamp song so perfectly shadowy David Lynch might be fond of it'. It was a track Adele worked on more than some. Having laid down the vocals, she later decided to re-record them – her perfectionist streak hard at work. Another change of heart was the song's position in the track listing: it was originally destined to be track four but was ultimately moved to the second place. It has become a favourite at Adele's live shows.

The stomps and full-on attitude of 'Rolling in the Deep' and 'Rumour Has It' vanish in 21's next offering. For 'Turning Tables', she teamed up with Ryan Tedder and recorded the track in London with Jim Abbiss. There are various stories about how she was inspired to write 'Turning Tables'. One of them is that she arrived at the studio one day in a mood after a row with her partner and something she said inspired Tedder. 'I didn't known Ryan at this point and I turned up going: "Who the fuck does he think he is, always turning the fucking tables on me?"' she told Digital Spy. 'And then he took that "turning tables" and came up with the phrase, which I loved.' The result was a song that was free of the stomps of tracks one and two. It was gentler but still had a palpable defiance.

In a variation on the theme of its genesis, Adele has also said the idea for a song about turning tables came after she had a row with an ex outside a Chinese restaurant in New York. They had been eating dim sum as their difference of opinion got out of hand. 'We stormed out into the street and kept turning everything round on each other,' she said. The lyrics are a clarion call from Adele in which she vows to be stronger, braver and more independent in future.

After he had recorded it with her, Ryan Tedder was listening back to it later that night. He sent her a message to share the emotional effect it was having on him. 'I'm sitting here listening to your song and I'm covered in goosebumps from head to toe,' he recalled during an interview with the BBC. In her swift reply, Adele said 'I am so glad you feel that way because I am sitting in my flat listening to this song and I can't stop crying.'

Musically, 'Turning Tables' would have fitted onto 19 and the same can be said of the opening of the next song. Produced by Rick Rubin and co-written with Dan Wilson, 'Don't You Remember' is a curious song to have on 21 because musically it initially feels more like a track from

19 before morphing into a very *21*-sounding song, while thematically its wistfulness makes it more like a *25* song. In it, she looks back wistfully at a recently ended relationship.

She remembered how a moment of embarrassment made her yearn to look back at a relationship more positively. 'I suddenly got really ashamed with the manner in which I was portraying someone who was really important to me,' she said. She added that she felt 'bad and childish' that she'd 'made them out to be a complete twat'. This made her remember the better times, when he would touch her and her skin would 'tingle'. She would also 'wait by my phone going crazy because he didn't text me back within ten seconds'.

The track 'Don't You Remember' has what Adele describes as a 'country tinge'. She adds that it is 'very American' and 'has a key change at the end'. It surely does have a key change – a massive and powerful one. This was a song that would connect well with US audiences. Overall, said Adele, the song is as an 'ode to a new discovery for me'. MTV said that 'ironically, this is one we will definitely remember'. However, you cannot please them all: the *Observer* was less impressed – its reviewer called the song a 'ghastly, mid-paced ballad'.

Next up is a song that few have done anything except gush over – 'Set Fire to the Rain'. Adele said the contradiction in the title of this power ballad is supposed to mirror the complexities of relationships, where 'one person says this, the other person says that'. For instance, she explained, 'I was heartbroken when I met who the song's about, and he brought me back to life and put me back together, and he was a dickhead as well'. However, in a more Adele take, she told BBC viewers before a performance of 'Set Fire to the Rain' that the title 'doesn't really make sense, but don't worry!'

Typically for Adele, she has offered other angles on how the song came about. She has said it was a reaction to a friend who told her that 'Chasing Pavements' was not enough of a gay anthem. In another story, she said it was conceived on a rainy day when her lighter wouldn't work because it was 'so wet'. Critics accuse Adele of myth-making, but, in reality, all of these stories could be true at once. Although people like to think that songs emerge from a single eureka moment, they are often influenced by a number of moments over what can be a long period of time. Moreover, there is no shame in artists putting a bit of spin on how they wrote a track – frequently the true stories are ones that would send many to sleep.

The paradoxical title of 'Set Fire to the Rain' echoes 'Chasing Pavements' from 19. One cannot set fire to rain, nor chase pavements, but this is the poetic beauty of both titles – they leave the interpretation open to the listener. In order to produce songs that can move so many people, the artist often has to leave a lot open to the ears and mind of the listener. While Adele can successfully deliver straightforward lyrics –

'Someone Like You', for instance, needs little decoding – she can also be more mystical.

'Set Fire to the Rain' was written with Fraser T. Smith. They had a good way of working together: Adele sat drinking coffee and drafting lyrics, while Smith worked on a piano riff. There were funny times in the studio. She had brought her dog, Louie, with her, and at one point it was feared that he might blow the studio up when he was chewing on cables.

'He Won't Go' was written with Paul Epworth and produced in Malibu by Rick Rubin. It is about sticking with someone even if you are told to leave them. The syncopated rhythm in the chorus makes this a very catchy song that stays in your head a long time after you've listened to it. She was inspired to create this song by meeting a heroin addict. After she had toured 19, she settled into a new flat and made new friends through their mutual love of dogs. One of her new group was a heroin addict, set for rehab. 'Their bond with each other overcame everything that was going on and that really touched me and moved me,' she told Digital Spy. In a happy coda to the story, she added that the man had been clean for a year and that she found it 'quite exciting' to see his new life develop.

Although Adele's material is often compared to artists from long ago, this track has been compared to more recent rhythm and blues acts such as Mary J. Blige. *Rolling Stone* said that 'He Won't Go' conjured an 'old-school/new-school magic act'. It was once considered as the track to close the album before they opted for 'Someone Like You'. As with *19*, they went for a big song to bring the curtain down on the album.

The song 'Take It All' emerged quite organically during a two-day session with Eg White. 'He played a chord, and then I just started singing it … and literally as I sang it, the lyrics sort of happened,' Adele said. 'I was really surprised about the contents. I only find out what I'm thinking and feeling in my songs. And I didn't realize I was feeling like this.' In this, the first song to be written for *21*, which therefore served as a bridge between *19* and *21*, she asks why everything she can offer is still not enough. 'It's about my devotion to someone, and them not caring, and taking the piss out of me, and exploiting me, in a way,' she said. Adele waited a few days before playing it to her boyfriend. 'He left me a couple of weeks after,' she remembered. They had been bickering a lot, she said, over everything from her lighter running out of fuel, to not putting enough sugar in a cup of tea.

'I'll Be Waiting' is more cathartic and upbeat, and very much fills the brief Adele set herself of composing more songs to dance to. Musically, it has been compared to everything from Aretha Franklin to the Rolling Stones. Its use of brass is glorious, and Adele said she had great fun recording it. 'Every time we added something new to it, or wrote a new part, we got really excited because we were happy,' she told Digital Spy.

Lazy commentary about Adele has it that all of her material consists of either angry or sad songs. She only ever rages at or sobs over her past partners, it is claimed. However, several songs disprove this notion, and 'One and Only' is one of them. This bluesy banger is one of her more optimistic numbers. It was produced by Rick Rubin. 'It's another happy song about someone that I've known for years,' she said in an interview on YouTube. 'We've always liked each other and never been together, even though I'm pretty convinced I'm probably going to marry this guy in the end. It's cheesy, but whenever I hear the bridge, it is sort of like that. I just imagine being kissed and the whole world slowing down and it being a bit like a fairy tale.'

Greg Wells, her co-writer for 'One and Only', gave a simple but powerful account of the song's composition. *American Songwriter* magazine quoted him saying, 'I heard a piano progression of four chords, and a slow six/eight feel. I kept playing it for about ten minutes. Adele was pacing the room with a note pad and a pen … then she finally said "I'm not sure if this is good but what do you think of this?" And then in full voice she sang the finished chorus and I almost fell over.' It's such a beautiful song that you cannot help but admire its hero. It's lovely to hear her sing so happily of him. However, Adele has since said that she has changed her feelings about the man the song is about, describing him as a 'fucking prick' and a 'knobhead'. Another in a litany of down-to-earth soundbites from a woman with a way with words in both song and conversation.

'Lovesong' is a cover of a Cure track, taking her back to that childhood gig when Penny took her to see them in Finsbury Park. Its inclusion is, therefore, something of a tribute to her mum. However, as Adele acknowledged, she felt under pressure to get it right, out of fear of Penny's reaction if she fluffed it. 'She'd disown me if she didn't like it, but she loved it!' Adele told *Variety* magazine. Indeed, Penny was incredibly sceptical about the proposition when she first heard of it, but once she heard the recording itself she was won over.

In fact, Adele has strict rules for attempting cover versions. Her early singles included covers on the B-side, but to include one as an album track seemed a bigger deal. 'I think it's really important that ... you either make it better than the original or you just make it a completely different song,' she said of covers. 'Lovesong' has also been covered by American rock band 311, recorded for the soundtrack for the film *50 First Dates* and been released as a single.

Rick Rubin had form here: he had been working with Barbra Streisand on a bossa nova-style cover of the Cure track. He took a similar path with Adele, and the outcome is a much moodier and mellower take than The Cure's original. Speaking of the original version, The Cure's lead singer, Robert Smith, told *Far Out* magazine, 'It's an open show of emotion. It's not trying to be clever.' Adele had also wanted to suggest another cover, of INXS song 'Never Tear Us Apart'. It was one of the first songs she had learned to play on the guitar as a child. However, when she played her version to Rick he felt that she sounded 'unconvincing'. Adele was devastated at first, but her successful take of 'Lovesong' helped to make up for the disappointment.

The album ends with her best-known track to date:

'Someone Like You'. This song came into being when Adele had just learned that her ex had become engaged to someone else just months after they had broken up. Could she have known what an impact this song would have on her existence? It has, and continues, to have a mammoth influence. 'It changed my life,' she has said. 'And every time I sing it, it changes a little piece of me.'

For Adele, this was the song she had been looking for. It was *the* song – that standout track that would define the 'Adele sound' and her career itself. 'I didn't have that one song that I believed myself on; that one song that moved me,' she said. 'It's important to me that I have that.' She began work on just that song at home, strumming on her acoustic guitar. Then, she took it to Dan Wilson, who quickly realized that this one had to be handled carefully and correctly. 'We didn't try to make it open-ended so it could apply to anybody,' he told *Billboard*. 'We tried to make it as personal as possible.'

The song that would become a talisman for Adele was recorded in a small studio on Santa Monica Boulevard in Los Angeles. This would prove to be an influence, too. Wilson told *Star Tribune*, 'It's a place with a high ceiling and a beautiful piano that I love … very simple and unglamorous, I think the space really affected the song and obviously the recording.' He remembered that 'by the end of the second day we had finished a demo, which I realized was pretty amazing … and that's what they used on the album'. He added that 'when she sings, there's just the thinnest veil between us and her emotions, in the room where she's singing, it's pretty hair-raising'.

Initially, Wilson envisaged that the final version of 'Someone Like You' would be a huge production, complete with strings and a choir. Ultimately, they realized that just the sad piano chords would be perfect. When Adele played the first take to her manager and mother, she recalled, Dickins loved it and her mother cried. Penny told her that this song would fix hearts across the world.

For Adele, writing 'Someone Like You' was as important personally as it was professionally. 'If I don't write a song like this, I'm just going to end up becoming a bitter old woman, forever,' she said. 'It was about putting us at peace, and coming to terms with the fact that though I'd met the love of my life, it was just bad timing.' That said, she was clear that she did not want to stay hung up on what they had had. 'I can imagine being about forty and looking for him again, and turning up and he's settled, he's got a beautiful wife, and beautiful kids and he's completely happy, and I'm still on my own,' she told the Page Six website.

However, she was realistic enough to note that 'the relationship summed up in "Someone Like You" changed me in a really good way', and reflected that 'it's made me who I am at the moment'. She rated the song at that stage as 'the favourite song that I've ever written, because it's so articulate' and 'completely sums up how I felt then'. She said she thought she would never write a better song than 'Someone Like You' and that it would be 'her song' forever. Perhaps she will better it one day, but if she does not, that will be no bad thing. To have this as your standout track is truly incredible.

The album closes on such a different note to the one it started with: from the foot-stomping defiance of 'Rolling in the Deep' to the gentle sadness of 'Someone Like You', with its perfect pairing of Adele and the piano. Adele said that when she wrote the latter song she was 'exhausted from being such a bitch, with "Rolling in the Deep" or "Rumour Has It"' and 'really emotionally drained from the way I was portraying him'. She told *Vogue* of the man the song is about: 'I had to write it to feel OK with myself and OK with the two years I spent with him. And when I did it, I felt so freed.'

When it came to the release of *21*, the experience was markedly different to the promo rounds for *19*. Although Adele had quickly achieved a level of recognition when her debut album came out, for *21* she was a star in much demand. Everything was cranked up and Adele could measure, here, how far she had progressed. As we have already seen, when Adele gives interviews she is often uncensored. Compared to those celebrities who have been media-trained to within an inch of their lives, Adele speaks freely and hilariously. Particularly in the early years of her career, she was blunt and amusing. Her answers could be streams of consciousness, wildly steering the conversation in different directions. She kicked off a promotional interview with the *Observer* by talking about her 'on-going colonic struggle with IBS', the right way to cook steak and the way that London smells – quite the combination.

The interviewer, Tom Lamont, said that her language during the interview had been consistently industrial. 'Assume, by the way, that Adele is swearing at all times,' he wrote. 'Between words, between syllables, she effs as easily as she laughs, and it would not be easy putting Adele, as Adele speaks, into print.' He also remembered that 'you're never quite sure where she'll go' with her answers. To demonstrate the point, he wrote that when he asked her about the difficulties of getting up for early morning TV appearances, she quickly landed on this passage: 'I love a card. You know, cards? At birthdays? I collect them. There's this place in London, in Soho, does the best cards. Upstairs. My friend took me, she knows I love a card. Downstairs. A sex dungeon. Oh mah gawd, the toys. All my best mates are gay, they love it. I've seen things – nuffink like this. My eyes were watering.'

Meanwhile, the reviews for 21 were always going to be an unpredictable prospect, but there was little to make Adele's eyes water for the wrong reason. Whereas for 19 the critics were assessing the debut album of a newcomer, by the time 21 came out they were dealing with an accomplished artist who had put out her (difficult) second album. 'There's cheating, jealousy, joy and heartbreak contained within,' purred the *Guardian*, 'all stripped into shape by a galactico squad sheet of producers'. Will Dean, the reviewer, singled out 'Someone Like You', writing that 'the tale of Adkins facing up to the end of a love … is half heart-wrenching, half uplifting – it's nearly good enough reason to break up with someone, simply so you can mope in it.' He said 21 was 'a progressive, grown-up second collection'.

However, over in the *Independent*, Andy Gill was unmoved, complaining that *21* has too many 'dreary ballads' and too much 'overwrought delivery that does her few favours'. Gill complained of a 'mire of turgid, characterless piano balladry swamped in routine string arrangements'. The *Daily Telegraph*'s Bernadette Mcnulty noted that *21* is 'steeped in Southern blues, country and soul' and 'Atkins makes the material sound genuine, largely because it is perfect for her'. She added that, on *19*, Adele's 'slight, observational songs seemed barely able to carry her powerful voice', but on *21* 'the emotional and musical heft of these styles enables her to really spread her vocal wings'. Praising Adele's 'warmth, power and vulnerability, sometimes in the same note', the critic said Adele had 'a voice that seems to go right to your heart'.

'At times, Adele's precocious talent feels prematurely aged by her material,' wrote Leah Greenblatt in *Entertainment Weekly*, 'and moments of levity are hard to find'. But Greenblatt concluded that 'at its best, *21* is that rarest pop commodity: timeless'. *21* is 'frontloaded like a steamroller sent to flatten all memory of her debut', felt the *NME*'s Chris Parkin, who loved the 'roiling gospel thump' of 'Rolling in the Deep' and 'Rumour Has It'. However, he only felt moved to award the album six stars out of ten.

Rolling Stone's Will Hermes said that on *21* 'Adele has toughened her tone, trimmed the jazz frippery and sounds ready for a pub fight.' Giving the collection three and a half stars out of five, he concluded that 'when the grooves are fierce, Adele gives as good as she gets'. Jon Pareles for

The New York Times praised Adele's emotive voice and compared her to Dusty Springfield, Petula Clark and Annie Lennox. He said Adele 'can seethe, sob, rasp, swoop, lilt and belt, in ways that draw more attention to the song than to the singer'. However, Allison Stewart of the *Washington Post* gave Adele a combination of compliment and insult when she concluded that many tracks on *21* were remarkable 'only because Adele is singing them'. Take that how you want to. In the *Chicago Tribune*, Greg Kot adjudged the music an improvement over *19*, writing that '*21* beefs up the rhythmic drive and the drama of the arrangements'. Steve Jones in *USA Today* said that Adele 'continues to distinguish herself with this stirring follow-up to 2008's *19*', a follow-up in which 'heartache and pain fuel her songs'. He noted that 'this scorned woman has the grit and sass to navigate a maelstrom of emotions'.

Barry Walters of Pitchfork website wrote that on *21* 'she wails harder and writes bolder, piling on the dramatic production flourishes to suggest a lover's apocalypse'. A fan of the album, he concluded: 'If you're looking for a record that'll make you wanna trash your beloved's belongings and have make-up sex amid the ruins, *21*'s your jam.' Margaret Wappler of the *LA Times* wrote, 'Who knows what damage she'll exact for *30*.'

As for Adele, she celebrated the release with an intimate performance at The Tabernacle in Notting Hill. She was not acting like someone whose new album was about to break countless records and catapult her to the very heights of fame. Instead, in her between-songs banter, she was an open book, embarking on the breadth of topics she had managed during that *Observer* interview. She told the crowd that she had stalked Kevin Costner at the CMT awards, confided that she loved Leona Lewis so much that she had spent nearly £100 voting for her on *The X Factor* and said that some of her acrylic nails were stuck in her guitar. The next morning she reflected how nice it had been to play in London again. 'I had such a brilliant time,' she wrote on her blog. 'I was nervous, excited, teary but over the moon!'

Then it was over to France for a TV performance in Paris. It proved quite a trip: thrillingly, she was given a police escort afterwards to make sure she reached the final Eurostar train that night. 'I felt like Whitney Houston meets Obama,' she said of the memorable experience. Back in the UK the following morning, she performed a Live Lounge session for BBC Radio 1. She sang four tracks from *21*, two from *19*, and a cover of Cheryl Cole's 'Promise This'.

Less than twenty-four hours later and Adele was performing 'Rolling in the Deep' on the *This Morning* show on ITV. She told the hosts, Ruth Langsford and Eamonn Holmes, that it 'went sour' with the ex who had inspired the album. One reviewer of the performance noted that 'Adele feels like an opened window on the sweaty bus of popular music. There's no artifice, no bullshit and little trace of ambition. Adele just does what she does, but she does it better than anyone else. And that's all we need right now.'

Commercially, the album was to prove an absolute juggernaut. It topped record charts in more than thirty countries and became the world's best-selling album of the year for both 2011 and 2012. In doing so, it helped boost the global music industry at a time that the sector was in dire need of a commercial behemoth to give it a lift. In the UK, it is the best-selling album of the twenty-first century, the fourth best-selling album of all time, and the best-selling album by a solo artist of all time. Thanks to its twenty-three-week reign at the top of the UK Albums Chart, it is the longest stayer there by a female solo artist. 21 also became the first album in UK chart history to reach sales of 3 million copies in a calendar year, and it is the most downloaded album in UK history.

In the United States, it is the best-performing *Billboard* 200 album of all time, holding the top position for twenty-four weeks, longer than any other album since 1985 and the longest by a female solo artist in *Billboard* 200 history. It was certified Diamond by the RIAA, marking sales of over 10 million copies in the US. It was the first album to be the best-selling album two years in a row since Michael Jackson's *Thriller* in 1983 and 1984. In February 2013, 21 reached two full years on the *Billboard* 200, never placing lower than 35 on the chart. Later, *Billboard* ranked 21 as the Number One album of all time on the *Billboard* Top 200 Albums of All Time.

The song that stood out for so many people was 'Someone Like You'. Here, she had really tapped into something that almost everyone could relate to. 'It's sad but beautiful and displays Adele at her best,' said MTV. The BBC said it placed the listener 'in one of those moments where you feel you're in the presence of a future standard'. Despite its relatively low-key production and musical simplicity, the song packs a potent emotional punch.

The music video for the track was filmed in Paris, France, by English director Jake Nava. 'The location evokes style and romance,' he said. 'And shooting early in the morning allows you to focus on Adele in this lonely and emotional space.' The video begins with a sad-looking Adele walking down a road alone. As she starts singing, the camera takes in Paris locations such as the Eiffel Tower. By the time of the second chorus, Adele stops singing and pauses on the Pont Alexandre III to gaze out over the Seine.

She continues to stroll through the deserted streets of Paris before finally reaching a building in which she spots her ex-lover. After seeing her, he starts to walk away and several shots follow of Adele looking at him. A reviewer said the video is 'a perfect match for the song's jaw-dropping emotional range – raw and unfiltered and incredibly sad but also, in a lot of ways, beautiful and resolute'. Amanda Dobbins of *New York* magazine described it as a 'secretly devastating' video. However, AOL's Ashley Percival described the video as predictable, and said 'It's all very pleasant, but after all this time, what's the point?' Certainly, Adele's promotional videos have rarely seemed remarkable affairs, nor felt like they were important to her.

Perhaps the most palpable testimony to 'Someone Like You' came at the BRIT Awards on 15 February 2011. James Corden, the host, set the scene with a pertinent introduction. 'There's nothing quite like the feeling when you're listening to a song written by someone you don't know, who you've never met, who somehow manages to describe how you felt at a particular moment in your life,' he said. 'This next artist is able to do that time after time. It's for that reason that she's currently Number One in an astonishing seventeen countries. If you've ever had a broken heart, you're about to remember it now. Here, performing "Someone Like You", it's the beautiful Adele.'

This was the song that had already taken Adele's fame to even higher levels. On the night itself and, thanks to a viral YouTube video, long beyond, the performance made jaws drop. At the end, James Corden said: 'Wow. Wasn't that amazing? You can have all the dancers, the pyrotechnics, laser shows you want but if you sound like that, all you need is a piano. Incredible.' It had certainly been a different experience to that of her first BRIT Awards. Then, she had been an unknown artist who was the first winner of a new gong, one that some industry figures were suspicious of. Adele must have known that some people felt she was being over-privileged by the honour. However, this time she was simply imperious. With their performances on the night,

Take That, Plan B and even Rihanna could not hold a candle to Adele. Everyone was speaking about only one thing: how amazing she had been. The performance has gone down in the history books as one of the very greatest BRITs moments.

This would not be the last time she would stand out at an awards ceremony. In the future, she would continue to hoover up awards at galas on both sides of the Atlantic, though arguably none of her performances at ceremonies would be as iconic as this one.

But for now, she was the Queen of the BRITs. No other artist was going to dare try and mock her this time, as they did in 2008. Instead, they all metaphorically knelt at her feet. Robbie Williams and Kylie Minogue stopped what they were doing to watch from the side of the stage. The cheers of the audience afterwards were described by one person there as akin to 'the roar of a thousand lions'. The *Guardian* said it was a 'virtuoso performance' that 'entranced and enchanted the arena'. The BBC News website said that 'while the O2 has ample capacity for pyrotechnics and casts of thousands in BRIT performances, the simplicity of Adele's song – just a flawless live vocal accompanied by piano – had guests on their feet'. The *Daily Telegraph* said she had 'knocked everyone for six with no bells and whistles – just a piano, her gorgeous voice and a monster song'. The *Mirror* said simply that she 'stole the show'.

A separate article by the BBC said this was a 'career-defining, reputation-sealing, sceptic-crushing performance'. The author of that article, Will Gompertz, remembered being present for a soundcheck in the same venue on a separate occasion. 'I was on my own save for seven or eight events staff preparing tables for that night's BRIT Awards,' he wrote. 'I was standing at the end of the runway stage when Adele walked on from the wings with three or four backing singers, tapped a microphone, signalled to the sound desk, and let rip with "Rolling in the Deep".

'Her voice filled the arena, its natural ampage sufficiently voluminous to make the great hall feel like an intimate nightclub – a sensation heightened by the raw emotion she conveyed in the song.'

On the night of such a key performance, some artists would have capped their triumphant show by partying hard, but that evening this was not on the cards for Adele. 'I've been on a detox, man!' she revealed on ITV2. 'Five days without fags, I'm five days clean! I ain't drinking, I ain't smoking, no fizzy drinks, no sugar, no dairy, no spicy food, no citruses ... no bloody nothing! I haven't been well so I've been very boring tonight,' she said. 'I've had laryngitis so I'm not even supposed to be – talking, never mind singing. It's rubbish – no drinking, no talking and no partying.'

It had been an evening that changed her life. Having been on a steady ascendancy for so long, this night proved an acceleration that made her soar into an even wider public consciousness. She moved from being famous to that most precious of positions – the household name. Remembering her iconic BRITs performance, Adele had more personal thoughts on her mind. She said: 'I was really emotional by the end because I'm quite overwhelmed by everything anyway, and then I had a vision of my ex, of him watching me at home and he's going to be laughing at me because he knows I'm crying because of him, with him thinking, "Yep, she's still wrapped around my finger,"' she said. 'Then everyone stood up, so I was overwhelmed.'

'It's really bizarre, at the BRIT Awards I was so frightened,' she said later. 'I've never actually been so scared in my life but it ended up being the most life-changing night of my life. Everyone stood up. I've never been given a standing ovation by my peers and by the industry. It was amazing. I was really embarrassed when I was singing that song because I hate getting emotional about my ex-boyfriend. I'm fine about it now but I realized in that four minutes that actually I'm not fine about it. That's why I broke down. I saw my manager and he looked proud and I love making him proud.'

She made her record company proud, too, because the adoring viewers sent 'Someone Like You' straight to the top of the charts. The song had not even been in the Top Forty before her appearance, but after the BRITs it went straight to the top, meaning Adele had two songs in the Top Five simultaneously – 'Rolling in the Deep' was at Number Four. Jonathan Dickins was so happy. 'She's made a great record that we're immensely proud of,' he said. 'And it's just another step in a long, fruitful career. Everything we try to do – every decision – is absolutely focused on the long term.'

Looking back at 21 with the benefit of a degree of distance, Adele likes what she sees and hears. 'I do love it. I just love the vibe of it … and I think some of the songs on here are the most articulate I've ever written.' But the irony is that, in a way, Adele wishes she had never written 21 – or at least the 21 that emerged. 'I don't think I'll ever forgive myself for not making my relationship with my ex on 21 work, because he's the love of my life,' she said.

Meanwhile, as her fame was soaring, the tragic death of Amy Winehouse was about to elevate Adele's celebrity to ever higher highs, as the attention of the industry and public turned to her. 'I got really famous right as Amy Winehouse died,' she told *Vogue* later. 'And we watched her die right in front of our eyes.' She added that Winehouse's death 'really offended' her. She explained: 'I picked up the guitar because of Amy's first album. She means the most to me out of all artists. Because she was British. Because she was amazing. Because she was tortured. Because she was so funny. I'm not having these people I don't know take my legacy, my story away from me, and decide what I can leave behind or what I can take with me.'

Noting how alcohol was so central to Winehouse's downfall, Adele began to reflect on her own relationship with drinking. 'I've always had a very close relationship with alcohol. I was always very fascinated by alcohol,' she said. 'It's what kept my dad from me. So I always wanted to know what was so great about it.' However, she found that different characters come out when you're drunk and the press would soon appear, sensing trouble. 'They descend, and descend, and descend on you, which drives you fucking mad,' she said. Perhaps this unease was behind her tame behaviour on the night she ruled the BRITs.

More than anything, those around Adele personally and professionally were determined that she would not stumble down the same path as Winehouse. When the 'Rehab' singer died she was twenty-seven, and much was made in the media about the fact that several music stars had died at the same age. Brian Jones, Jimi Hendrix, Janis Joplin, Kurt Cobain and Jim Morrison were all twenty-seven when they died. Although there was no suggestion that Adele was living a life that was likely to send her to an early grave, there was still a strong sense that she needed as much support as possible.

'It's a death trap, this industry,' she told the *Daily Telegraph*. 'I mean, you play to two thousand people who adore you, then you go back to your hotel room alone. That's quite a comedown.' As for drugs, she insisted, 'I've never taken an illegal drug in my life. I want to be known for my music. I don't want to be in the press for having coke up my nose, because my nan will see it.'

Thinking more of Winehouse's downward spiral, Adele admitted, 'I do worry about it … it's easy to fall into. I don't do drugs, I've never done a drug in my life, but I'm a big drinker. And when I do a show and I've got six hours to kill, I just get drunk because I'm bored. So I can see how it

LEFT: With her trusty acoustic guitar, Adele performs on the MTV2 stage at the Great Escape Festival, Brighton, May 2007.

RIGHT: Her first BRIT – the Critics' Choice Award – came in February 2008. This moment launched her into public consciousness.

BELOW: At the piano rehearsing with Jools Holland before a live performance on his *Later With …* show in March 2008. She had watched the show as a child and was thrilled to be invited to perform.

ABOVE: With David Bowie and Iman at Keep a Child Alive's 5th Annual Black Ball in November 2008.

LEFT: Stunned as she collected the Best New Artist GRAMMY – one of four of the awards given to her first album, *19*, that night in February 2009.

ABOVE: (*l-r*) Jordin Sparks, Adele, Leona Lewis, Miley Cyrus and Jennifer Hudson, at the VH1 Divas concert at Brooklyn Academy of Music in September 2009, held to raise money for the Save the Music Foundation charity.

RIGHT: Refusing to let her newfound celebrity go to her head, Adele chose an intimate evening at the Tabernacle in Notting Hill, London, for the launch of her second album, *21*, in January 2011.

ABOVE: At the BRIT Awards 2012, Adele accepted the Best Album award from one of her musical heroes, the late George Michael.

BELOW: With Simon Konecki at the 54th Annual GRAMMY Awards in Los Angeles in February 2012.

could happen.' She has also said that 'coke is everywhere', in the music business. 'It would be so easy to fall into it. I am an addictive personality: if I start something I don't stop. I smoke thirty cigarettes a day, I drank a lot in the past. I know I would go on to other things and I don't want that.'

Even without drug use or excessive drinking, when Adele was twenty-one she did face a true emotional crisis and needed to draw on the support that was around her. She was 'really falling apart', she told *Vogue* years later. Noting Adele's turmoil, her mother moved back in with her daughter to give her stability and support. 'She lovingly put me back together,' said Adele. 'I was missing her a lot,' she added. 'It's nice just to hear her there. There's a really long hallway and her room is at the other end but just hearing her pottering about is really comforting. And it's nice to have someone to come home and make a cup of tea for when you've been away for ages.'

Again, Penny's loving role in Adele's life can hardly be overstated. Adele has referred to Penny as her 'best friend' and regularly credits her with a role in her success. 'We are thick as thieves,' Adele told *The Scotsman* newspaper. 'She's the love of my life. She doesn't worry about little things. She's never disappointed even when I know she probably is. You know that parent thing, "I am not angry; I am disappointed." Like a bullet. She's not like that.' In 2013, Adele reportedly gifted her mother a £600,000 Notting Hill property as a thank you for everything she had done for her during her life and career. Whether it is support for her professional or private life, Penny has been generous and loving to her daughter.

Meanwhile, Adele was also proving quite a storm across the Atlantic. The US public were fans of her music and she enjoyed a breakthrough there that many UK pop stars could only dream of. However, her American dream would be darkened by a cancellation that showed again how she struggles with the demands of fame and which foreshadowed an even greater US crisis much further down the line.

CHAPTER FOUR

BREAKING THE US

When she was fifteen, Adele had gone to New York with her father. She was so excited. During that visit, a seed was sown in her mind. 'I remember going into the massive Virgin store in Times Square where I thought how amazing it would be to one day have a record in a record shop abroad,' she said, in an interview quoted in the *Daily Mail*. However, such an ambition is easier dreamt of than done, because although the US is sometimes referred to as the land of opportunity, it is more often the land of failure for overseas musicians. As the *Independent* once put it: 'It has become something of a tradition for any successful British band to try their luck across the Atlantic, only to return after a year with their tails between their legs as the American audience refuses to acknowledge their genius.' Oasis, Robbie Williams and the Spice Girls were acts frequently held up as examples of this.

So, Adele had many reasons to doubt whether she would break the US market before she even spoke to her team about the prospect. Her manager, Jonathan Dickins, laid it on the line for her. 'I'm learning about the US all the time – but it's a very difficult market to break,' he remarked. He explained that of new artists who broke through in America, ninety-seven per cent of them were domestic, compared to the UK, where just forty-nine per cent were domestic. 'That gives you an idea of how hard America is,' he told Music Business Worldwide website.

Although the US is a nation with a ravenous appetite for power ballads by soulful women such as Shania Twain, Diana Ross and Whitney Houston, Adele's accent would prove another challenge. Her urban, sassy London pronunciations were part of her charm for UK ears, but for the ears of those in America's Deep South and Midwest, it was a different story. So the questions that were being asked in her camp were whether this would be an obstacle for her and, if so, whether she should compromise her inflections or stay true to her roots. She set out determined to not change. She told CNN: 'I'm not like, some, like, blonde, skinny, fake boobed, white teeth, really stupid. I'm nothing like that, and I think that appeals to people. I hope that I never start looking like a Playgirl.'

There was one more reason why the US market was going to be a challenge for Adele to crack: she hates flying. She worries that the plane will crash without her even getting a chance to phone her loved ones to say goodbye. That sort of anxiety makes getting to the US hard, but also makes travelling within that vast continent a challenge as, without flying, this would be a time-sapping experience.

Her quest to make it in America began on 17 March 2008 at Joe's Pub in New York. In many ways, it was a humble event. There were just 184 people in the audience at the Lower Manhattan venue. Tickets were just $12. Yet this evening was to prove auspicious, launching her in the US. As she arrived on stage, with just one spotlight lighting her up, she had more than one reason to be nervous: she had caught a slight cold since her flight and her team had put honey in her tea backstage. 'Forgive me if I start coughing up or something during a song,' she said, with a laugh.

The success of her US debut can best be summed up by the fact that by the time she performed at the venue again the following night she had signed her US record contract. The deal was a joint venture between Columbia Records and XL Recordings for *19* to be released in the US. Her first major US write-up came on 19 March in the prestigious *New York Times*. It wasn't particularly favourable. Nate Chinen wrote that Adele 'presented two distinct personalities ... on the one hand she was the self-assured performer' but 'on the other hand she was a jittery teenager playing her first show in the United States, with a head cold'. The review described Adele as 'professionally impudent' and an 'overqualified coffeehouse act rather than a budding pop star'. As for the songs themselves, Chinen felt they were 'poised but callow'. America would soon be lapping up the emotional depth of those 'callow' songs.

Not the most glowing of reviews, but it got Adele's name out there. Shee already had a very influential champion in the US media in the form of show-business blogger Perez Hilton. With millions reading his posts, Hilton had the power to launch any new act if he gave them his approval. He did just that for Adele, writing that she had a voice like honey. *Goldmine* magazine, too, was positive about her, with its reviewer remarking that 'I have just seen a star in the making, and I will not soon forget that performance'. These early champions were a huge help to Adele as she tried to crack the US.

Her third US show was at the Hotel Café in Los Angeles. In the audience was Alexandra Patsavas, an influential figure in US TV. As a result, two months later, 'Hometown Glory' was played during an episode of the US medical drama series *Grey's Anatomy*, taking it to new levels of public recognition. Then came her An Evening with Adele tour, which saw her booked to play fifteen venues across the US and Canada. One such show was at the Bonnaroo Music and Arts Festival in Tennessee. *Rolling Stone* said of the confident performance: 'During her hour-long set, she showed off her huge, Aretha-style pipes. Most impressively, the twenty-year-old seemed totally unfazed by her performance.'

For the tour date, she typically opened shows with 'Cold Shoulder', before belting out 'Melt My Heart to Stone' and 'Daydreamer'. She would eventually finish the main body of the set with 'Hometown Glory', before re-emerging for a three-track encore, which climaxed with 'Chasing Pavements'. The presence of 'Hometown Glory' in the set must have been emotional for her as she was indeed missing home. 'I'm sitting in a car park for trucks in between Minneapolis and Ann Arbor and am feeling very homesick,' she wrote on her blog. 'I miss my mum and my friends Brett and Clyde.' She later wrote about a 'horrible' tour bus that she was forced to share with 'six stinky guys' and a blocked toilet. Tours of the US might sound glamorous from a distance, and in many ways they are, but there are some grubby moments, too.

One of the last performances on the tour took place at the Hollywood Bowl, an iconic venue that was named one of the ten best live music venues in America by *Rolling Stone* magazine. Adele's hero Etta James was supposed to appear at the show, but she cancelled at the last-minute due to illness. She was replaced by Chaka Khan. Adele's opening acts for the shows included The Script, James Morrison and Sam Sparro. After the tour she published an official tour book containing exclusive pictures and behind-the-scenes information.

But amid the glamour and the grubbiness, Adele was determined to make it work. 'She wants to work it properly, and put in time there,' XL CEO Richard Russell told *Billboard* magazine. 'People are really excited about her over there.' She was not naïve about the scale of the task, as she explained herself. 'Well, obviously the US is a lot bigger and there is a little more work involved,' she said. 'There's politics: if you do one thing, you can't do another thing; you don't do this and you won't get that. That stuff doesn't exist in the UK. I guess because there are so many different kinds of markets in the US, you need to define your niche. I think that's probably it. You can't go to America and be shit; you could have an amazing figure and they won't buy it,' she said. It is talent alone that matters there, she insists. 'I could wear a bin liner and they'd still like me.'

She was being booked onto the top TV shows, the sort of slots that most artists could only dream of. 'Yeah, I did *Letterman* and *The Today Show*,' she told Digital Spy. 'I had no idea what they were the equivalent to because obviously we don't have them here. I was like, "What's *The Today Show*?" and they were like, "Imagine GMTV but on a much bigger scale." It was live and there were like 50 million people watching so I literally just s**t myself! *Letterman* was pre-recorded so I wasn't quite as nervous, but I forgot that during my performance. I got halfway through the song and couldn't remember whether it was live or not. Look it up on YouTube – you'll see my face just drop!'

Along the way, she did promotional interviews aplenty, following the media demands of the project. Before long, she was noting the way that US journalists would ask slightly different questions to those asked by the reporters she was used to speaking with in the UK. 'I knew people would ask me – especially here with the whole Hollywood thing – if I felt pressure to lose weight,' she said. 'I don't think it is important. I think it used to be more important, and I think there are aspects of it now where people will talk about what you look like, not what you're doing. I made a record. I don't want to be on the front cover of *Playboy*. I want to be on the front cover of *Rolling Stone* with my clothes on.' After the tour, she said, 'I was a bit scared when my American agent said he was going to put me on a fifteen-date tour over there, but thanks to the power of the internet people showed up at my gigs and knew all the words and it all went amazing.'

The power of the internet had already helped her, and now the power of luck was going to have its own influence. In October 2008, she appeared on *Saturday Night Live*. It proved to be a career-changing moment. She had been booked after a producer from the show saw her perform live in Manhattan. 'It was just meant to be like a normal show,' said Adele. 'Then we walked in on Saturday and Sarah Palin was there!' The presence of Palin, a divisive Republican politician and vice-presidential hopeful, put Adele's episode of *Saturday Night Live* on a whole new level as viewing figures soared as high as 17 million viewers – its biggest figure for ten years. Amusingly, Adele mixed up Sarah Palin and Tina Fey backstage, as she explained later. 'I f**king love Tina Fey, and I was, "Tina, Tina". She didn't even acknowledge me, she was just completely oblivious. She was really nice backstage, but I'm one hundred per cent chuffed to pieces that Obama won,' said Adele, who had been wearing an Obama badge backstage. 'I'm not a fan of her – at all.'

Suddenly, the worm was turning. After the show finished, *19* was downloaded by tens of thousands of people, launching it to Number One in the American download charts. It also reached Number Five on the Amazon charts, and 'Chasing Pavements' hit the Top Twenty-five. Writers, too, began to take more interest in her. 'For two months now, I've been causally listening to *19*,' wrote an *Entertainment Weekly* reviewer. 'But it took two powerhouse performances on *Saturday Night Live* to make me truly appreciate this cheeky (yet quite stage-frighty) pile of cuteness ... suffice it to say that now I love Adele even more.' The *Richmond Times* said: 'So was she worthy of the prestigious musical slot on a show that attracted 15 million viewers? You betcha.'

To capitalize on the success of her appearance on *Saturday Night Live*, Adele quickly announced plans to head back to the US for a new, eleven-date tour in early 2009. During this tour she blogged that it had been 'amazing' and full of 'jokes' and 'Coca-Cola'. The first date was in Somerville, Massachusetts, where a reviewer remarked that Adele sang 'with such sincerity ... that it felt like she was singing only to you'. The final show was at the Art Deco Wiltern Theater in Los Angeles, where anticipation was building: the $25 face-value tickets were changing hands online for more than ten times that. *Variety* magazine said the concert delivered, as its critic said that the show convinced that 'she has many different avenues to take on a second record'.

Adele's US stock was growing in value all the time. She was invited to appear on the American comedy-drama series *Ugly Betty*. The series centres around the character Betty Suarez who, despite her lack of style, lands a job at a leading fashion magazine. Adele was handed a cameo role in the episode 'In the Stars'. She said, 'Very nice to meet you', and

'Ta-ra, take care', and performed her song 'Right as Rain' to promote her album *19*. The episode aired on 14 May 2009, but Adele admitted that she was not blown away by her performance. 'I'm the worst actress of all time,' she said. 'I'm like a fucking cardboard box.' At least her fans could rest assured that she was not about to switch to being an actress.

The more she appeared on American television, the more invitations she got to appear on American television. On 10 June, when *19* was released, Adele appeared on the NBC morning programme *The Today Show*. She sang 'Chasing Pavements' but changed the lyrics to 'chasing sidewalks', to fit in with the US vernacular. However, as she later explained to *Blues & Soul* magazine, there was no way she was going to go further and actually change the song's title. 'Chasing pavements is a very English phrase that a lot of Americans don't get,' she said. 'A lot of people have even suggested I change the title to "Chasing Sidewalks". But I'm like "Fuck off! I ain't changin' for you! I'm from London."' That pressure to change both her words and the accent she sang them with was going to have to be a lot greater before she would even consider surrendering to it.

This self-confidence and boldness served her well and she had plenty to be proud of when she looked back at her early ventures in the US. 'I actually feel it's not that hard to break America,' she said. 'It's just a case of you have to be there and have the stamina to keep going back and forth. Because … if you show commitment then everybody wants you. And I actually think the reason why a lot of people don't break America is because they can't be away from home for that long. I know that for me America is definitely going to be a slow-build situation.'

It should be noted that sales of *19* in America did prove to be slow initially. She arrived back in the US in September, played in New York and enjoyed a handful of broadcast appearances. But the album was not selling spectacularly, as one US paper noted. 'The album arrived in June and throughout the summer moved about 80,000 copies – not a shabby showing for a newcomer in this brutal state of the music industry,' it said. 'But that big breakthrough, the one that her level of talent deserved, wasn't happening.'

Looking back, she reflected on when things started to change. 'It must have been on *Saturday Night Live* when Sarah Palin turned up, and Alec Baldwin and then Marky Mark – who isn't really my era, but my mum loves Marky Mark, so I sent her a text, and my aunts love him too,' she said. 'The whole year's been a bit random, the fact that [*19* has] done so well, all the time I'm like "What's going on?" It's a bit bizarre, but I wouldn't change anything for the world.'

She was asked whether the dramatic events of that year had sunk in. 'I don't think it ever will,' she told Digital Spy. 'It's all gone so fast that it's impossible to notice everything that's happened, let alone take it all in. I tried to develop a tough skin for a while and kept ignoring everything that was going on, which made me come across a bit confrontational and cocky I think. But in fact I'm the complete opposite: I couldn't be happier with what's happening, but I'm trying not to think about it in case I s**t myself.'

Another, less dramatic, but nonetheless significant, development during 2008 was that Adele started to cook for herself. Back home in the UK, she tried out some relatively easy dishes first, such as chilli con carne and stir-fries. Then she moved to the slightly more challenging lasagne. Having invited Penny over for dinner, she said, 'I'm going to attempt to do a proper Christmas dinner with loads of roasties and those little sausages with bacon wrapped round them – I love them.' However, if Penny was hoping for a real Christmas tree to eat by she would be disappointed. 'I've got a fake Christmas tree 'cos after a while I think the real ones smell like piss,' said Adele.

When Adele found out she had been nominated for four GRAMMY Awards in 2009, she was in shock. She had not expected to be nominated for any. At first she heard that she was named in three categories, but within minutes her manager called to confirm she had been nominated for four: Best New Artist, Record of the Year, Song of the Year and Best Female Pop Vocal Performance. 'It was Adele, Adele, Adele, Adele,' she recalled. 'I never thought in my wildest dreams with my first record that I'd be included.'

'I was screaming,' she added, remembering that crazy evening. 'I had to put the phone down. It was the proper death of me. I didn't think anyone would ever really care until my third or fourth record, so I wasn't bothered that [my label] thought it was a long shot. My manager came over to my house at, like, four-thirty in the morning with a bottle of champagne that I'd bought him in September for his birthday because he's ... cheap.' Even a week later she was still struggling to accept the news. 'I'm waiting for someone to say, "You mug, we're only joking!"' she said. This suggests an element of imposter syndrome – the internal experience of believing that you are not as gifted as others perceive you to be – was at work in the back of her mind. In truth, a big part of her felt it was too soon for her to win a GRAMMY. 'It's like [actors who win] an Oscar too soon, it puts a dampener on the rest of their career.'

She wanted to look her best on the night, so she turned to *Vogue* style guru Anna Wintour, which shows she was definitely not suffering from an excess of imposter syndrome. Adele spoke to Wintour at her *Vogue* office when she was the subject of a photo shoot there. 'It was just like *The Devil Wears Prada*,' Adele said, citing the novel and film that are based on Wintour. 'I got a really nice dress. I don't ever wear dresses. I wear dresses with tights and flat shoes and a cardigan. But I am going to get my boobs out and everything. It's going to be quite a big deal.'

Barbara Tfank, an American fashion designer, who is best known for designing the lavender Prada gown worn by Uma Thurman at the 67th Academy Awards, had been lined up by Wintour to put together an outfit for the singer. 'Adele came to my office,' Tfank remembered. 'We sat down at a table and I said, tell me about when you're onstage and how you like to feel and how you like to look. She had this very cool beehive hair from the night before and that inspired me, too.'

Adele had been anxious before the *Vogue* encounter but was soon put at her ease. 'Anna Wintour was lovely,' she told *Grazia* magazine. 'Nothing like I'd feared before I met her. I was expecting Meryl Streep in *The Devil Wears Prada*. Anna was wonderfully articulate and really friendly. She turned me into a lady, and she introduced me to Barbara Tfank who made my GRAMMYs dress, and who has continued to make me pieces for videos and shows, and more recently my outfit for the Royal Variety Performance.'

Finally, the big night of the GRAMMYs ceremony in Los Angeles arrived. When Adele went on stage to collect her Best New Artist award, she commiserated with the other nominees. She said, 'Thank you so much. I'm gonna cry … Duffy, I love you, I think you are amazing. Jonas Brothers, I love you as well.' She also won Best Female Pop Vocal for 'Chasing Pavements', to the joy of mother Penny, who was watching from Adele's flat. The singer had suggested her mother watch from there, so she could 'smell' her and feel close to her. Naturally, Adele phoned her as soon as she could on the night, whereupon Penny ticked her off for chewing gum as she collected an award.

Adele described the whole evening as 'like an out-of-body experience'. She said she didn't expect to win anything and described the moments of victory in a charming and down-to-earth style. 'I was sitting between Coldplay and U2 at the front,' she told the *Daily Mail*. 'When they called my name out, I was expecting to be asked to move to the back. I wasn't expecting to be on stage. My belt was undone, my shoes were off and I was chewing gum. On my way back down, I nearly walked straight into Chris Martin.'

There was a surreal moment backstage when Adele encountered Justin Timberlake but did not realize at first that it was him. 'In the hallway after I'd won two GRAMMYs, he grabbed me and he's like, "Congratulations,"' she recalled. However, she added, she was 'so totally overwhelmed about the GRAMMYs that I didn't even realize it was Justin'. She continued: 'Then, ten yards down the huge hallway in the Staples Center, I just heard this huge scream and realized I was screaming my head off.' Any fears that the evening had gone to her head were eased when Adele gave another characteristic interview backstage. 'I'm going to go and put my jeans on ... and go and have some cigarettes and hang out with my manager and my friends,' she said. All in all, Adele had approached the evening as a rookie who could not believe her luck, rather than a diva who expected to be automatically crowned.

Not that this humble air could save her from scrutiny. Just as when she won her first BRIT and faced criticism, including from Arctic Monkeys, Adele was questioned by some after her GRAMMYs triumph. The soul singer Estelle asked, 'How the hell is there not a single black person in the press singing soul?' Speaking to the *Guardian*, she added, 'Adele ain't soul. She sounds like she heard some Aretha records once, and she's got a deeper voice – that don't mean she's soul. That don't mean nothing to me in the grand scheme of my life as a black person. As a black person, I'm like: you're telling me this is my music? F*** that!'

Adele responded – but not with any anger. 'It's an opinion and I like people with an opinion, so if that's what she thinks then fine,' she told Digital Spy. 'She doesn't listen to me like Aretha, but you know I didn't ask her to, so whatever. I'm sure it was a bit misquoted – people always misquote people and I know that, but whatever, I don't care. I'm doing my thing and she's doing hers.'

Back in the UK, she was asked how it had gone in America. 'Amazing – and it's all so unexpected,' she said. She celebrated her return to Blighty with a 'four-day bender' in London with her friends. 'I love my friends so much that I do get quite moody when I'm away from them,' she told Digital Spy. 'It was five weeks this time which is quite a long time, but the shows were so good that it made up for missing them.'

Between March and September 2011, she set out on her second major concert tour. The shows took in several European countries and North America. She was backed by a five-piece band and backing singers, although for some tracks she was accompanied by piano only. The set-list was a true crowd-pleasing one: she would typically sing all songs from 21, except for 'He Won't Go', and a handful of tracks from 19.

Rob Sinclair, the production designer, wanted to focus the attention of the shows onto Adele and her voice. So he set out a sparse set. That said, the show was not without its spectacular moments. At some gigs, a 20-foot mirrorball descended from the ceiling during the encore and during 'Hometown Glory', an image of St Paul's Cathedral was projected onto a screen. The encore was powerful, comprising of 'Someone Like You' and 'Rolling in the Deep' – the two tracks the audience craved more than any.

The front-of-house engineer for the tour, Dave McDonald, had a similar attitude to the rest of the team – the shows should be an absorbing and diverting experience. 'I want the audience to forget who they are for a moment and be able to project themselves solely onto what's occurring onstage,' he told ProSoundWeb website. 'That is, after all, why we go to shows.'

This focus on Adele's voice, rather than on pyrotechnics or the other theatrical distractions that many other pop idols would use on stage, was justified and admirable. However, the greater that focus on her voice was, the more pressure it put on Adele. She not only had to be in a certain place at a certain time, she had to be 100 per cent on her game. This was a scary, as well as exciting, experience for Adele and that anxiety did not disappear.

Indeed, for all her highs on the road, Adele has suffered some enormous lows when it comes to live shows. In October 2011, she was forced to scrap a ten-date US tour because of a vocal cord haemorrhage. Announcing the cancellation, she wrote on her blog: 'Guys, I'm heartbroken and worried to tell you that I am yet again experiencing problems with my voice ... I follow all the advice I am given and stick to regimes, rules and practices to the best of my ability, but it seems to simply not be enough.'

Within weeks, she was forced to cancel all her remaining live dates and promotional appearances for the rest of the year, and announced she would have to undergo throat surgery. News of the surgery worried Adele's fans. It worried Adele, too. She had been live on a radio station in Paris when she felt a pop in her throat, 'as if a switch had been flicked'. Her voice quickly went deeper and she knew something was wrong. Just how wrong was the subject of much speculation. Rumours circulated that she had cancer and that she might die, but a specialist doctor, Dr Steven Zeitels, put it all into perspective when he told *Rolling Stone* magazine that he didn't believe the problem was serious. 'It's very fixable, basically,' he said. 'This is not something that's a deal-breaker, even remotely.'

Speaking to the *Sun*, Adele said it was not her singing that was the problem. 'I damage my voice offstage, not onstage,' she said. 'Onstage I am fine as apparently I am technically great, but when I talk I damage my voice big time. I have got screwed into giving up smoking. If I wasn't a singer I still would be smoking twenty-five a day.' Although she made light of the issue, Adele must have wondered whether the worst would happen and she would not be able to ever sing again.

In November, she confirmed that the throat surgery had proven a success. Having undergone laser microsurgery in the US, she thanked her fans for wishing her a speedy recovery. 'Thank you for all your positive thoughts and get-well wishes,' she posted on her official blog. 'I'm doing really well, on the mend, super happy, relaxed and very positive with it all. The operation was a success and I'm just chilling out now until I get the all-clear from my doctors.' She noted that 2011 had been 'the most erratic year ... fucking brilliant and exciting and emotional'. She was, she added, ready for a break – she wanted to take some time out and 'just be' for a while. However, she announced, she would 'be back' and 'I'm gonna smash the ball out of the park once I'm touring again'.

Later, it was reported that Dr Steven Zeitels, the director of the Massachusetts General Hospital Voice Center, had indeed performed a procedure to 'stop recurrent vocal cord hemorrhage from the benign polyp'. Dr Zeitels had form: he had previously performed the same surgery on other singers, including Aerosmith frontman Steven Tyler, Lionel Richie, Cher and Roger Daltrey from The Who. He was the man who had pioneered the procedure, which uses specialized lasers to stop vocal-cord bleeding in singers, so she could not have been in better hands.

Adele flew back to the US in January 2012 for the moment of truth: had the operation been a success, or was her time as a singer over already? Dr Zeitels examined her throat and was encouraged to see that it seemed to have healed. However, the proof would be in the vocal pudding. After his examination of Adele, Zeitels asked her to sing. She chose her hit 'Rolling in the Deep' for this special, intimate performance. He was delighted and relieved by her performance, which was, he felt, even better vocally than before the operation. He said he felt an 'overwhelming epiphany' that he had restored 'this beloved voice that would bring joy and inspire millions of people'. Needless to say, Adele was rather pleased herself with the outcome.

She was also pleased when she found out she was up for six GRAMMYs in 2012 including the three most prestigious awards: Best Album (21), Best Record and Best Song of the Year (both 'Rolling in the Deep'). Adele found it mindblowing to be nominated for six awards, and felt that to win all six would be beyond her wildest dreams. But as the *Guardian* put it: 'Adele is the kind of English woman Americans take to their hearts' because 'she's comfortable with her body, glamorous without being intimidating and seems thankful for the gift of her smoky voice, and the rewards it has brought ... in short, she's wholesome without being dull'.

It felt fitting that Adele dominated the awards on a night when the ceremony was also dominated by the recent death of another imperious songstress, Whitney Houston. 'We've had a death in the family,' said the evening's host, the hip-hop star LL Cool J. 'It feels only right to begin with a prayer for ... our fallen sister.' There had been another tragic recent death: of Adele's heroine Etta James. Indeed, Adele had paid tribute to James on her website. 'What a lady Etta James was,' she wrote. 'She was the ultimate original. Her voice was breath-taking and her songs are reflections we all recognize in some way or another. It's an honour every time I hear her voice ... Thank you to Etta James.'

Adele looked magnificent on the night of the GRAMMY Awards, with a classy black dress and a lighter hair colour. When she picked up the award for Best Solo Performance, she paid tribute to Dr Zeitels and his team, saying, 'Seeing as it's a vocal performance, I need to thank my doctors, I suppose, who brought my voice back.' Her acceptances are often entertaining, during one of them at the Staples Center, she said: 'Mum, girl did good!' However, perhaps most memorable was her acceptance for the GRAMMY Album of the Year. She was in tears as she accepted it and remarked, 'Oh, I've got a bit of snot.' From chewing gum to snot, she was changing as each GRAMMY win came along.

However, it was her singing voice that there was most anticipation for on the night. Gwyneth Paltrow introduced Adele's performance, saying that 'singular voice of hers' was back. It was indeed: as if to underline her confidence in her vocals, Adele chose to begin 'Rolling in the Deep' a cappella – with no instruments to hide behind. Then the band joined in, and Adele was imperious. No wonder everyone from Rihanna to Sir Paul McCartney were openly agog with admiration. This was as close as she has come to equalling her 'Someone Like You' performance at the BRITs.

She later looked back on what she wore at the GRAMMYs: a custom Giorgio Armani dress that was designed with sequins and a black mesh overlay, paired with diamond earrings and bold red lipstick. During an interview with *Vogue* in 2021, she said that outfit was her most iconic fashion moment. 'And I was pregnant, so I just love that dress,' she said.

She felt triumphant that night and had proved a winner for the US audiences. For most British pop acts, trying to crack

America was like pushing water uphill. Adele had reached the top of that hill and was enjoying the view. Hidden, and almost forgotten, among this stateside success, was a sadder episode. Adele had been due to fly to the US for some live shows and promotional activities in 2008. However, she did not want to leave her then boyfriend, 'Mr 21', and so she demanded that all of those commitments were cancelled so she could stay at home.

Her initial statement blamed the cancellation on family issues. 'There's some problems at home I've had to sort out,' she claimed at the time. 'I was looking forward to touring and throwing myself back into it. But my home life needs more attention. I apologize from the bottom of my heart for disappointing you all.'

Although the statement was somewhat vague, it was difficult to take issue with her reasoning in those words. However, a year later she got more specific and honest. 'I couldn't bear to be without him,' she said of Mr 21, 'so I was like, "Well, OK, I'll just cancel my stuff, then."' Looking back, she said, she found it hard to believe how she had behaved. 'It seems so ungrateful,' she told the *Nylon* digital magazine.

This incident and her words about it would feel so much more significant in 2022, when she dramatically, and mysteriously, cancelled her Vegas residency. Cancellations have become a feature of Adele's career, and while she has been increasingly condemned for them, it should be noted that she is more exposed than arguably any other act currently on the live music circuit.

CHAPTER FIVE

MUM'S THE WORD

t was early in 2011 that the idea first emerged for Adele to record a James Bond theme song. Sony Pictures President of Music Lia Vollack suggested to the Bond team at Eon Productions that they ask her to record the song for their next Bond film, *Skyfall*. Vollack had reasoned that the 'soulful, haunting, evocative quality' of Adele's voice would bring back the 'classic Shirley Bassey feel' associated with the Bond franchise's early years.

This is the sort of honour that many singers dream of, but it is also a challenge. At first, Adele was not keen. She had just brought out *21*, with all the drama and demands that an album release entails, and felt a 'little hesitant' about the Bond idea. She told the movie's director, Sam Mendes, that she was the wrong choice to write and sing a Bond theme because 'my songs are personal, I write from the heart'. The gulf in the emotional potency of her recordings of her own songs, and her recordings of covers, bore this out. Although she realized she would be involved in the writing of any

Bond track she recorded, she worried there would still be too much emotional distance.

Mendes took her point but felt it was a bit simpler than that. 'Just write a personal song,' he said, suggesting that she use Carly Simon's 'Nobody Does It Better' from *The Spy Who Loved Me* as an inspiration. He handed her the script to *Skyfall* and told her to read it and give the proposal some more thought. After she had read the script, Adele 'fell in love' with the film's plot and decided that it was a 'no-brainer'.

Paul Epworth, with whom she had worked on *21*, helped her write the track. They took their time over the process, analysing past Bond films and soundtracks in search of a common thread they could grasp hold of. Epworth told the *Financial Times* he had a eureka moment when he identified 'a minor ninth as the harmonic code'. Known by musicologists as the 'big daddy' of the three 'prime dissonances', the minor ninth is a compound musical interval spanning thirteen semitones (one semitone more than an octave) and is often used to add tension to music. It did that brilliantly in 'Skyfall'. He told the BBC that he and Adele wanted the romance of the lyrics to reflect Bond's relationship with his country and MI6.

Despite reports that she had recorded the entire song in just ten minutes, Epworth later clarified that she had only recorded the first draft of the verse and chorus in that short period. However, he was full of praise for her, writing on Twitter that 'she had great finesse and skill' and was more than 'just a powerhouse'. According to Epworth, the song's lyrics are about 'death and rebirth'. He said: 'It's like, when the world ends and everything comes down around your ears, if you've got each other's back, you can conquer anything. From death to triumph, that was definitely something we set out to try and capture.'

The song was previewed with a ninety-second clip on Adele's website on 5 October 2012, which was Global James Bond Day. It was also the fiftieth anniversary of the release of the first Bond film – *Dr No*. 'Adele paces herself carefully, delivering her vocal with understatement and restraint but gradually powering up as drums, strings and horns kick in,' wrote Neil McCormick in the *Daily Telegraph*. 'She waits till the final notes to give it the full Shirley Bassey, dragging out the last "skyfaaaaaaallll" for thirteen seconds.' *Entertainment Weekly* cheered that there is 'finally' a great James Bond theme, while the *Huffington Post* described the song as a 'brassy and soulful tune that fits perfectly alongside the work of Shirley Bassey in the oeuvre of James Bond title tracks'. The *Guardian* was also impressed, with Jude Rogers writing that 'her delivery reveals the best of Adele: the sound of an ordinary girl capable of extraordinary feeling'.

In the US, the *Los Angeles Times* said that the song was 'not a reimagining or a musical departure, but simply a righting of the ship ... it is big, bold and seems to have a little spot-o-fun'. MTV purred that 'Adele's lush song fits right in with classics by Shirley Bassey, Paul McCartney and Carly Simon.' The most important verdict came from James Bond himself, the actor Daniel Craig, who said he cried when he first heard the song. 'From the opening bars, I knew immediately,' he said. 'Then the voice kicked in and it was exactly what I'd wanted from the beginning. It just got better and better because it fitted the movie. In fact the more of the movie we made, the more it fitted.'

The praise for 'Skyfall' was immense, but just as pertinent for Adele was the context. The release was heralded as a massive moment in music, significantly beyond the sort of rapturous hype with which a Bond theme by most artists would be greeted. There had been quite a build-up of excitement. In September 2012, OneRepublic vocalist Ryan Tedder posted a message on Twitter claiming he had heard the track and declaring that it was 'the best James Bond theme in my lifetime'. Adele's publicist, Paul Moss, mentioned the song on his Twitter feed, but both men later deleted their social media messages. As excitement and speculation built, the artwork for the song was leaked online, but Adele's involvement in the project was not officially confirmed until 1 October.

However, it curiously did not reach Number One in the UK. Rihanna's track 'Diamonds' kept it off the top spot. Nevertheless, it initially tied with Duran Duran's 'A View to a Kill' as the highest-charting James Bond theme song on the UK Singles Chart. The two acts' joint record has since been broken: in 2015, Sam Smith's 'Writing's on the Wall' for the film *Spectre* went one better, debuting at Number One on the UK Singles Chart. Over in the US, 'Skyfall' entered the *Billboard* Hot 100 at Number Eight for the week ending 20 October 2012, becoming Adele's first song to debut in the Top Ten. It reached Number One in several territories, including Belgium, France, Germany, Hungary, Israel and South Korea.

Having recorded the song for Bond, who works for Her Majesty's Secret Service, in 2013 Adele was awarded an MBE for services to music by the Prince of Wales at Buckingham Palace. It was a proud and surreal moment when she was introduced in the palace ballroom as 'Miss Adele Adkins'. She stepped forward with a wide grin. She shared a few words with Prince Charles before he pinned the award on her black, long-sleeved Stella McCartney tea dress and shook her hand. Adele then stepped back, offered a little curtsey and, walking away, had a hearty chuckle to herself. In a statement released after the ceremony, she said, 'It was an honour to be recognized and a very proud moment to be awarded alongside such wonderful and inspirational people. Very posh indeed.'

The MBE was exciting, but Adele had had even more thrilling news. When the time came for recording 'Skyfall' she was heavily pregnant. The song has a low range musically and this helped her nail the vocals in her expectant state. According to a study by the University of Sussex in 2018, women's voices drop by an average of two notes when they are pregnant, because the volume of extra fluid near the vocal cords causes them to vibrate at a slower than normal rate.

Therefore the song was a good fit for Adele, and the father of her child seemed to be a great fit, too. When she got to know Simon Konecki, Adele quickly decided she would be a 'fucking damn fool' to walk away from him, not least because she considered that he would be the perfect father for her first child. Some were surprised when they learned that Adele and Simon Konecki were an item. An Old Etonian man might not have seemed the obvious match for a Tottenham girl with left-wing leanings. Konecki had Polish roots, as his grandfather, Leonard, was born there during the First World War. Leonard and his wife eventually settled in England, where Simon's father Andrew was raised, going on to work in the City of London. Simon's birth, on 17 April 1974, was announced in *The Times*.

Simon spent part of his childhood in the US after the family moved to New York. After they returned to the UK they sent Simon to Eton College, the elite boarding school in Berkshire that has educated establishment figures such as William Pitt the Elder, Prince William and Boris Johnson. Simon was in the house that had the naughtiest reputation in the school. 'Our headmaster used to refer to him as the naughtiest boy he had ever had in the house,' remembered a fellow pupil in the *Evening Standard*. 'Don't misbehave or you will end up like him,' the headmaster would say.

Another former pupil said of Konecki: 'He wasn't exactly a charmer. He had a terrible eighties' mullet and awful acne, and virtually my only meaningful exchange with him – other than plenty of classroom jibing – was when he taught me to smoke (badly) behind the rackets courts.' The source said that he was for a 'brief, nauseous moment' part of Konecki's gang 'but not for very long once he realized that someone aged sixteen who couldn't smoke a Marlboro Light properly was hardly going to be entourage material'.

One day at Christmas, the thirteen-year-old Konecki was walking through Brighton. He spotted a homeless man – or a 'hobo' as Konecki described him when recalling this memory for the *Financial Times* – and decided to give him the ten pounds he had to spend that day. 'When I got home my dad said, "You're crazy. He's just going to spend it on drugs." But I think he needed it more than I did that day.'

However, this seemingly rebellious childhood was not enough to stop him succeeding in adulthood. He moved to the City and started life in the Square Mile as a trainee foreign exchange banker. He had worn a pin-striped suit and red braces for the interview, hoping he would evoke Charlie Sheen's character in the *Wall Street* movie. He was teased for his attire, but he got the job. He went on to become a director of EBS, a division of trading giant ICAP.

Before long, he had lost his love of working in finance. 'I was doing well and earning a lot of money, but I got sick of that greedy and corrupted world,' he told *Management Today*. After leaving the Square Mile he set up a charity and moved to Brighton. He was married to his first wife, Clary

Fisher, and they had a daughter, Georgie, together. Friends say he would ride his black Vespa scooter to business meetings, conjuring the image of a Richard Branson-style character, full of energy, ideas and eccentricity.

He set up a company called Life Water, with the hope of providing an ethical alternative to bottled water. The aim was that every litre of Life Water sold would fund clean drinking water for communities in the developing world. This would be arranged by a charity Konecki had formed – drop4drop. Although he struggled at first, things looked up when he agreed a deal with the supermarket chain Waitrose to stock his product. He enjoyed trips to Africa and India where he could see his vision being realized.

However, by 2009, he was less happy: he and Clary had split up. In December 2011, Adele offered her first signal that she and Konecki were an item. In a rare tweet, she promised that she would tweet more prolifically in the future if at least 10,000 of her fans started following the drop4drop charity's Twitter account. The following month, Adele and Konecki were spotted together on holiday in Florida. They visited the Everglades National Park and watched for alligators near the beach.

When it was reported that Adele was dating a married man she was furious. 'This is the first and last time I will comment on the details of my relationship with Simon,' she wrote on her website. 'Contrary to reports and headlines in the press today, Simon is divorced and he has been for four years.' When she was interviewed on the *60 Minutes* television programme, she quipped that she did not want her relationship to end just so she could write another heartbroken album about the experience. 'I'm madly in love and I don't want to be, like, "Babe, I'm sorry we've got to break up. I've got a new album to deliver."'

For Adele, the equation was simple. She felt she had met the one – the one for her and the one for her future children. 'I was like: I'd be a fucking damn fool to walk away from this man being the father of my child compared to any other man that I encountered before or after up until recently, phew! I would've regretted that, forever!' she told *The Face* later. When she discovered she was pregnant she told friends and family but asked them to keep the news private for the time being. She called her grandmother, Rose Evans, to tell her but did not contact her father. Instead, Rose passed on the news and assured Marc that Simon was a good man. When Adele finally announced the news publicly, on her website, the statement was formal – almost akin to the sort of messages that the royal family releases at such times:

'I'm delighted to announce that Simon and I are expecting our first child together. I wanted you to hear the news direct from me, obviously we're over the moon and very excited but please respect our privacy at this precious time. Yours always, Adele. Xx.'

She and Simon were living in a nice mansion in a West Sussex village. Life felt good and it was about to get a whole lot more eventful: a son would be born, a knot would be tied and – in between those two bookmarks – a third album would be released.

CHAPTER SIX

25 – SMASHING RECORDS

There is a significant difference between arrogance and supreme self-confidence. Adele showed she had plenty of the latter when she went about announcing her third album. On 17 October 2015, millions of viewers were sitting down and watching *The X Factor*. In truth, the ITV talent show had seen its best days by this stage. There were still some contrived moments of drama, but it had been a while since anything genuinely exciting happened on the show. It continued to draw a fair audience, but many were watching more out of tradition and habit rather than from curiosity and excitement. They were hoping something exciting would happen.

So it was that, during a commercial break on that night's show, something very exciting happened. Without warning, a black screen appeared and an unmistakable voice sang 'Hello, it's me.' Viewers were not told or shown who was singing and that was the point – Adele's voice is so recognizable, and a new album by her had been so long awaited, that no explanation or context was needed. It was clear it was Adele and it was clear she was, finally, coming back. The nation rejoiced and social media was flooded by excited posts. It was a 'Yes' from Britain.

Thus began the promotional campaign for 25. The BBC later described the album's launch as 'straight out of Steve Jobs's handbook: control everything, withhold information, build up anticipation, never break cover, keep the message simple, and treat your product's arrival as if it is a major event'. There was no need to 'worry about feeding the wider media machine', it continued, because 'it will gorge itself quite happily on scraps'.

Sometimes things are worth waiting for. After she released 21, Adele served notice that it might be a while until the public saw or heard of her again. She said, 'I'll disappear and come back with a record when it's good enough.' In another chat, she put it more bluntly: 'I am fucking off for four or five years.' Even her most dedicated and impatient fans wouldn't want her to release an album that wasn't 'good enough', but how many could have predicted that it would take her four years to return?

Certainly her record label team were not as patient. As ever in this industry, what the money men wanted was a new product to sell. Their priority was income, not integrity. Adele was not about to buckle to their pressure. 'I won't come out with new music until it's better than 21,' she told them. 'I'm not expecting to sell as many records, but I don't want to release shit.' These were not the words that the money men necessarily wanted to hear. In May 2014, she seemingly announced a release of the album within months, when she took to Twitter and posted a photo on the social network, captioned: 'Bye bye 25 … See you again later in the year x.'

The run-up to the release was a long, slow-burning affair. Speculation began in 2011 over how her new album would sound, when Adele told Q, 'It won't be a big production. I want it to be quite acoustic and piano-led. I want to write it all, record it all, produce it all and master it on my own. I think it'll take a lot longer because I want to do it this way.' There were also rumours that the album would be her most country sound to date, while the grapevine suggested at one point that a reggae album was on the cards. That would have been an interesting diversion.

What happened during that long wait for her third album showed the dedication and attention to detail with which Adele approaches her work. The process began with a customary ritual. When she was ready to start work on the album, Adele walked to her local shop and bought a brand new notebook. 'I do it every album,' she explained to *i-D*. 'I buy a new pad, sniff it – 'cause smell is important – and then I get a big, fat Sharpie and write my age on the front page.' The moment she did that she was surprised to be reminded how old she was, so when she wrote twenty-five, she put five exclamation marks after it ''cause I was like, "How the fuck did that happen?!" Twenty-one to twenty-five.'

It was time to take the plunge. To get things rolling, she went to her friend Kid Harpoon's studio to try out some new music and see how it felt. It was 2013, and Adele found she was not ready yet. 'It was a "dip my toe back in the water" thing really,' she remembered. 'Me and [Kid Harpoon] get on great, so I went in with him 'cause I knew there was no pressure. We just chatted, mainly, and got chocolate tempura. I don't know why I wasn't ready, I just couldn't access myself.'

She took a break and then a few months later, she flew to New York and things started to get moving. She was working with Ryan Tedder, the OneRepublic frontman, a talent with whom she had some stunning form: together they had produced 'Turning Tables' and 'Rumour Has It'. This time, their sessions conjured a track called 'Remedy'. Adele was so pleased with the track, she got over-excited and thought 'I'm on a roll!', but, she admitted later, 'I weren't on a roll', for what happened next was that she 'started knocking out some shit songs' which were rejected by her manager. 'This isn't good enough,' Jonathan Dickins told her.

Adele appreciated his honesty but still admitted that this damning verdict on the early material knocked her confidence. So she flew Rick Rubin over to New York and played him the tracks, she told *Billboard*. What Rubin told her was the thing she most feared hearing. He said: 'I don't believe you.' She has admitted that her 'worst fear' is 'people not believing me'. So it was back to the drawing board, to try and find her mojo. Slowly, things began to improve and the beginnings of an album took shape.

Another early track from the sessions was 'Send My Love (To Your New Lover)'. This was a song that surprised a lot of people, with its cheeky, impish and almost calypso vibe. 'It's a bit of fun, innit? You ain't got to be dark all the time,' Adele told *i-D*. The song first emerged when she was just thirteen. She had bought the debut Amy Winehouse album, *Frank*, and felt inspired to pick up her guitar. 'If it wasn't for Amy and *Frank*, one hundred per cent I wouldn't have picked up a guitar,' she told online culture magazine *Mic*.

If Winehouse was the initial inspiration for this track (and all that came after it from Adele) then another globally famous singer-songwriter was also an inspiration. When she and Tedder were at lunch one day, they heard Taylor Swift's 2012 single 'I Knew You Were Trouble'. Adele loved the vibe and decided to work with the man who produced the track – Max Martin.

'I was like, "Who did this?" I knew it was Taylor, and I've always loved her, but this is a totally other side – like, "I want to know who brought that out in her,"' she said. 'I was unaware that I knew who Max Martin was. I googled him, and I was like, "He's literally written every massive soundtrack of my life." So I got my management to reach out. They came to London, and I took my guitar along and was like, "I've got this riff", and then "Send My Love" happened really quickly.'

It was recorded at two studios: MXM Studios in Stockholm and Eastcote Studios in London. The original title of the song from was going to be 'We Ain't Kids No More' but she changed it to 'Send My Love (To Your New Lover)', reasoning: 'Otherwise, you might as well just call the fucking album "*Old*".' The esteem in which she holds this taunting track is reflected in the fact that it was, at one stage, considered for the lead single off the album. However, it was felt that it did not embody the theme and content of the wider work, and they led with 'Hello' instead. Speaking to the *Guardian*, Adele referred to 'Send My Love …' as a 'fuck-you song' to an ex-boyfriend. It would go on to draw comparisons to Gloria Gaynor's 'I Will Survive' and Beyoncé's 'Irreplaceable'.

Slowly, things were coming together. She also sang with the legendary songwriter Diane Warren, as the American revealed in 2014. 'It was just great,' Warren told *Entertainment Weekly*. 'I don't really write with people and we spent a lot of time together and really clicked and really connected and I really like her as a person … I'm really excited about the stuff we did.' However, Warren conjured a more cautious note over the fate of the songs she wrote with Adele, saying: 'We did some great songs but I don't know if they've made the record. I don't think anybody does.' One thing Warren was certain of was that she was a fan of how Adele operates. 'She has a mind of her own,' said Warren. 'Nobody rushes Adele or makes decisions for her, which is probably why she's a great artist. She wants to get it right.'

Adele also worked with Greg Kurstin, who had won three Ivor Novello awards for his work on Lily Allen's album, *It's Not Me, It's You*. They met at the Metropolis Studios in Chiswick. The pop veteran Phil Collins was another to cross paths with Adele as she worked on her new album, but he was disparaging about his experience. 'She's a slippery little fish is Adele,' he told *Q*. Collins claimed: 'She got hold of me and asked if I would write with her. She gave me a piece of music to finish and at first I didn't know if I'd failed the audition as I didn't hear back from her. And now I've heard there's an album coming out. I'm not on it, I know that.'

Damon Albarn, the former lead singer of Blur and Gorillaz, also spent some time with Adele, and he, too, spoke a bit coldly of the experience and whether his input would be part of the album. 'I don't know what is happening really,' he told the *Sun*. 'Will she use any of the stuff? I don't think so.' He added, 'The thing is, she's very insecure. And she doesn't need to be, she's still so young.' Albarn added that some of the material he heard from Adele was 'very middle of the road'. It seemed a shame that Albarn and Collins both felt the need to swipe at her, not least because it made them appear rather old and dour.

Interestingly, Albarn would go on to face criticism for his sneering remarks about another successful female singer-songwriter. Talking to the *LA Times* in 2022, Albarn had replied to the interviewer calling Taylor Swift 'an excellent songwriter' by arguing that 'she doesn't write her own songs'. An angry Swift immediately responded on Twitter: 'I was such a big fan of yours until I saw this. I write all of my own songs. Your hot take is completely false and so damaging.' So that was him told.

As for Adele, swipes from the sidelines were not going to deflect her. She was determined to make the album she wanted to, and would do whatever it took to get there. 'For a little while I was quite frightened by it and getting into the headspace of writing a new record I found really difficult,' she said. She reported that she suffered from a block. 'I felt like this was never going to happen, I was never going to finish this record, it was a long process,' she confided to Nick Grimshaw on the BBC. 'I thought I ran out of ideas and lost my ability to write a song.'

Simply trying to produce a new 21 was not on the cards. 'I was very conscious not to make 21 again,' she said. 'I definitely wasn't going to write a heartbreak record 'cause I'm not heartbroken, but I probably won't be able to better the one I did, so what's the point? Bit cliché, innit?' In fact, she confided that there was a period when she considered calling it a day and making 21 her final album. She thought: 'Maybe I should just go out on a high? Maybe people have heard enough of me? Maybe that's all they want to hear,' because she 'didn't want to come back with anything that people wouldn't like'.

However, she recalled, her team was 'amazing' and they would tell her to 'go back to the drawing board if something wasn't good enough'. She said her 'biggest fear' throughout the writing process was that 'I wrote songs that I didn't believe myself', because her 'biggest thing is I want people to believe me'. Therefore, as her first words about the album in November 2013 showed, she was willing to take time over it. Speaking to reporters at the GRAMMYs, she said: 'I'm not very far along at all. I'm having lots of meetings. I've been out of the loop really. I've been singing my baby nursery rhymes, so I don't really know what's cool and what's not.' She said that she would be visiting Paul Epworth, who produced and co-wrote some tracks for *21*, including 'Rolling in the Deep', which boded well for the new material.

With the reggae rumour out of the window, the question was what the theme of the new album would be. 'It would be fucking awful if my third album was about being happily settled down and maybe on my way to being a mum,' she said. She didn't want to be that pop star who finds success and then writes about their new life, which is unrelatable to fans. 'I get annoyed when all singers write about is cars, limos, hotels, boring stuff like missing home, complaining,' she said. 'I have a real life to write about.'

Cynics assumed that the album would be simply a collection of break-up songs, but it turned out to be more varied than that. Indeed, it could have been radically more varied than that. She told the BBC's Nick Grimshaw: 'I did pretty much write an album about being a mum. But that's pretty boring for everyone. I scrapped that.' What eventually emerged was, she told the SiriusXM radio service, a 'make-up' album rather than a 'break-up' album. 'This record is all about how I feel as opposed to how someone else has made me feel,' she explained.

She did wonder if she'd taken too long – a year too long – in releasing the album. 'But you know, I was being a mum,' she told *i-D*. 'I couldn't rush it. And you've got to give people a chance to miss you.' People certainly had missed her, and when the album was finally released, her fans pored over the eleven songs that make up 25.

Speaking of 'Hello', she truly leant into the nostalgic flavour of it. 'I felt like a lot of stuff in my life has changed and not at all because of my career, but just because stuff changes as you get older,' she told the BBC. 'And I found myself yearning for my past for no reason other than it had gone and I missed elements of it. I didn't want to be back there, I just missed elements. I felt all of us were moving on again. It's not about an ex-love relationship, it's about everyone that I love.'

Speaking to *i-D*, she said: 'The song is about hurting someone's feelings but it's also about trying to stay in touch with myself, which sometimes can be a little bit hard to do.' She went on to explain: 'It's about a yearning for the other side of me. When I'm away, I really, really miss my life at home. The way that I feel when I'm not in England, is …' she paused, then went on, 'desperation. I can't breathe anywhere else.' Why? 'I dunno. I'm so attached to my whole life here. I get worked up that I'm missing out on things. So "Hello" is about wanting to be at home and wanting to reach out to everyone I've ever hurt – including myself – and apologize for it.' This is not the only song on 25 in which we can feel Adele's mixed feelings over how her fame has taken her around the world.

'Hello' is a piano ballad, laced with a bit of soul and a lot of gravitas. It took her six months to write the song and the time was worthwhile, given how beautifully and spookily the track renders the themes of nostalgia, regret and distance. As she told the BBC: 'I felt all of us were moving on, and it's not about an ex-relationship, a love relationship, it's about my relationship with everyone that I love. It's not that we have fallen out, we've all got our lives going on and I needed to write that song so they would all hear it, because I'm not in touch with them.' She has added that the 'other side' she sings of in the chorus refers to 'the other side of becoming an adult, making it out alive from your late teens, early twenties'.

She wrote 'Hello' with Greg Kurstin, who later spoke to *Vogue* about the experience of writing a song with Adele. 'She has this way of tackling very complex emotional subject matter that I've never seen,' he said. 'Also there's this commitment to a song idea, where if the opening line of a song resonates with her, we could be working on it over the course of years, just perfecting it. She pushes me to places that are very unexpected on the piano. Sometimes I'll be looping a progression for hours while she's figuring out the lyrics. It's almost like a meditation.'

The mood changes a lot for track two on 25. 'Just the guitar, okay, cool,' says Adele as 'Send My Love (To Your New Lover)' begins. The finished production of the track made it as upbeat and uptempo as it deserved to be. The nimble, playful atmosphere makes it a rarity not only on the album but in all Adele's material to date. Her most poppy and jaunty song, 'Send My Love …' is perfectly positioned in the album to make listeners sit up and take notice that 25 is worth listening to.

Co-written with Paul Epworth, 'I Miss You' is quite a different proposition. She wrote it in one night while lying on her bed. 'Whenever it's on, I always get hypnotized by the beat. That's just about the general intimacy of a relationship, she told *The New York Times*. 'It sounds very sexual, but it's not only sexual.' Asked by *i-D* if the song was about sex, she laughed and said, 'It's about intimacy on every level. It's about sex, it's about arguing, one of the most intimate moments in my life. 'Cause you just blurt it out. It's a bit like, a drunk tongue is an honest one. That's definitely my motto, in life. That's why I don't really like drinking no more. The panic you get when you wake up the next morning.' If those episodes influence songs as powerful and enchanting as 'I Miss You', many listeners will hope there are more of them.

Adele has often said that track four, 'When We Were Young', is her favourite song she has ever written, surpassing even the great 'Someone Like You'. Many fans would share that feeling, given the polished perfection with which this song emerged from the studio, like something from Elton John's heyday. This track, which she has said she considers as 'a letter to myself', is, she has added, very much the entire album in microcosm.

She worked on it with the Canadian-born singer-songwriter Tobias Jesso Jr. 'I was nervous as shit,' he later wrote about his experience of writing with Adele, but he soon calmed down in her company. 'I can tell from the bottom of my heart she means what she says and the words she puts into her music. Every lyric and every line comes from a place she feels. She doesn't settle.'

Speaking to American broadcaster Carson Daly, Adele said, 'It's just such a beautiful song and I wrote it with a great artist. It's about seeing someone that you haven't seen in so long. It's written in the future, like twenty years' time, and then you see this person and because so much time has passed and so much has happened to both of you, it's ridiculous. And you get on so great. It's just about enjoying each other in that moment.'

Ariel Rechtshaid's production on the track is particularly strong. 'He just nailed it, really,' said Adele. 'He nailed the production, 'cause I didn't want it to be subtle. I didn't want it to be a piano ballad. I wanted it to have a band, and I wanted each instrument to be a person at a party, you know. I wanted the bass to be like, that guy in the corner having a drink, and I wanted the tambourine to be some girl dancing like, by the stairs, you know, and Ariel really nailed that for me, so I was super chuffed.'

'When We Were Young' is a standout track not only on 25 but in Adele's entire canon. She flew to Los Angeles and recorded it on Philip Glass's piano, at Tobias's friend's nan's house in Brentwood. 'It used to be this mad party house and for some reason his piano was there so we wrote the song on that,' she said. *Rolling Stone* remarked that it 'may be the most wrecking of her parlays' into heartache, 'not because it recounts any particular instance of heartbreak but because in under five minutes, she spins the existential crisis-inducing topics of time and aging into what feels like a snapshot of our own past, present, and future'.

As we have seen, she wrote 'Remedy' with Ryan Tedder. *The New York Times* gave an insight into how it came about, noting of the song's composition that 'Mr. Tedder had the word "remedy," some waltzing piano motifs, and the idea that the song might be about someone beloved; he looked to Adele for the rest.' Tedder himself has said that when Adele told him the song would be about her son, Angelo, that 'unlocked the whole lyric'. Speaking about the song to *Rolling Stone*, Adele explained, 'I wrote it about my child. But I sang it for everyone that I really love. When I wrote it, I got my confidence back in my writing 'cause I believed in myself.' By the time of 30, these themes would become more commonplace in her work, but, at the time, 'Remedy' was a fresh foray for Adele.

'Water Under the Bridge', co-written with Greg Kurstin, takes her sound in another direction again. The mid-tempo track features an electro-drum beat and a trip hop riff. There is also a hint of eighties rock, fittingly enough for an album steeped in nostalgia for a distant past. However, lurking in the background of the sound is a gospel choir. Lyrically, it focuses on the pivotal point in a relationship, where you take stock and see where you stand. Although the chorus has a catchy, singalong vibe, this does not come at the expense of any intimacy. The chorus stays with you long after you have listened to it.

After the poppy sound of 'Water Under the Bridge', comes the mystical, almost ghostly melody of 'River Lea'. The Lea itself is a lengthy river, which emerges in Bedfordshire, in the Chiltern Hills, and flows south-east through Hertfordshire, along the Essex border and into Greater London, to meet the River Thames at Bow Creek. It has been a big part of Adele's existence, and she has many memories of it from her earlier years. 'A lot of my life was spent walking alongside the River Lea to go and get somewhere else,' she told America's NPR media organization.

The track was co-written with Brian Burton under his pseudonym Danger Mouse, and again a gospel note can be tasted in the production. Next to the comparatively light and frivolous sound of 'Water Under the Bridge', the water of 'River Lea' feels full of gravitas. The melody is almost ominous in parts. The river practically becomes a being, a character, as Adele sings so accusingly of the influence that her roots have had on her.

'The idea of the song is that, especially since I've become a parent, let alone writing this record, I'm dealing with myself for the first time,' she told NPR. 'And I have a lot of bad habits. And rather than admitting that I have bad traits in my actual character, I blame it on where I'm from.' Here, perhaps, we can sense the impact that life in Hollywood – where prim and proper West Coast Americans fear acting in any way that is deemed 'inappropriate' – has had on Adele, a cheeky and outspoken girl from London. As we have seen, Adele's sense of humour can be very lewd. One wonders whether she has said things that offended the more puritanical Californian attitude and ended up internally blaming it on her childhood, on her River Lea. 'There's a saying, you can take a girl out of Tottenham, but you can't take Tottenham out of the girl,' Adele told *The New York Times*. Well, listening to the glorious 'River Lea', why would you want to?

Perhaps the saddest song on 25, 'Love in the Dark' was co-written with her bass guitarist, Sam Dixon. One of the most generous of her heartbreak songs, here she is not raging against a man, but simply, sadly, accepting that what they once had is over. 'If there's one thing we know about Adele, it's that given the option to either remain stagnant for the comfort of anyone else or break free for the sake of what's best for herself, she'll always choose the latter,' said *Rolling Stone* of the track.

Written after she had driven past her old haunts in south London, the song 'Million Years Ago' is so yearning and nostalgic it could almost hurt to listen to it if it were not so beautiful. With a French feel, the song sees Adele lament her youth and yearn for the life she had before stardom. She sings that she misses her mum, her friends and everything else that seemed so normal before fame changed her life. She would later remark that she continued to miss south London. 'I used to love it,' she told *The Face*. 'I used to live by the bus station opposite on Tierney Road. And I used to love that walk in the morning past the fresh bakery, all that fresh bread, I loved it. My best friend Laura lived in Streatham for a while by Nando's, we always went to Nando's. We ate there every day.'

You get the sense that Adele is doing a lot of processing with 25, and here she is processing how it feels to be famous and to have lost what you had before. The received wisdom is that stars who sing about the downside of fame tend to lose their audience. Why would someone living an ordinary life in England relate to the woes of a superstar living in Los Angeles? However, Adele manages to explore such territory in a way that everyone can relate to. It's quite a skill.

'All I Ask' was co-written with Bruno Mars, but it is rooted in the pop music of the 1980s, before Mars or Adele hit the scene. It has been compared to big ballads of that decade, including Diana Ross and Lionel Richie's 'Endless Love', Peabo Bryson and Roberta Flack's 'Tonight I Celebrate My Love', as well as Phil Collins and Marilyn Martin's 'Separate Lives'. With 'All I Ask', the poppy, cheeky Adele and the ghostly Adele of previous songs is gone. This is perhaps the most 21-esque track on 25, complete with its beautiful late key change, which only succeeds in making Adele seem more vulnerable.

'Sweetest Devotion' is a love letter to Adele's son. Angelo can be heard at the start and finish of the song, in a manner less controversial than the appearance he would make on 30. Given that 21 closed with 'Someone Like You' and 19 ended with 'Hometown Glory', it is clear that Adele likes to leave an album's biggest song to the end. 'That's my son,' Adele told USA Today of 25's big finale. 'The song is all about my kid. The way I've described it is that something much bigger has happened in my life. I love it that my life is about someone else.'

Just as stars singing about fame in a relatable way is a tricky task, so is writing about the joys of parenthood without making the experience seem like the musical equivalent of being forcibly shown pictures of someone else's baby. The *Guardian* said the task 'is tricky enough to flummox even Stevie Wonder at the height of his powers' and described 'Sweetest Devotion' as 'sickly rather than bland'. So ends her third album. Given that her first two albums ended with huge songs, some felt that 'Sweetest Devotion' was a little lacklustre in comparison. However, overall 25 had delivered.

Which brings us to the critical reception for the collection. The more heavily an album is anticipated and the longer the wait for it, the more volatile reviews of it often are. Once the work finally emerges, the critics seem more inclined to either praise it to the hilt or to pan it. They know more attention than usual is focused on their critical assessment so they are quicker to offer eye-catching verdicts. With 25, there were indeed some extreme reactions – mostly at the positive end of the scale, but with a handful of negatives, too.

'Pop doesn't come more perfect than this,' said the *Daily Telegraph*'s Neil McCormick. Noting the mammoth anticipation that had built for the album, he wrote that: 'I don't think anyone will be disappointed' by 25, which 'is certainly the equal of its predecessor'. McCormick said the album was 'crammed top to bottom with perfectly formed songs' and 'elegantly flowing melodies, direct and truthful lyrics and richly textured production' which were 'all sung as if her life depends on it'. He felt he detected the influence of a cast of legends, including Lionel Richie, Phil Collins, Carole King, Burt Bacharach, Charles Aznavour and Enya. It all made for a great piece of work, for him. 'She loves to sing, and the world loves to hear her,' he concluded.

Noting the album's heavy load of nostalgia, *i-D* magazine said: 'It's about what was, what is, what might have been. It's about missing things that you had no idea were so precious, like being eighteen years old and drinking 2-litre bottles of cider in Brockwell Park with your mates.' Bruce Handy of *Vanity Fair* said 25 was the 'confessional blockbuster you wanted it to be'. Noting how much heartbreak Adele had been through to produce such rawness, he wrote: 'Poor Adele. I hope she can take comfort in the fact that, however blue she feels, anguish becomes her. She sings even her dopiest, mopiest lyrics with such force and conviction that, well ... you try resisting.'

Another positive verdict came from Jon Dolan of *Rolling Stone*. He wrote that the album's 'nostalgic mood' is the 'perfect fit for an artist who reaches back decades for her influences, even as her all-or-nothing urgency feels utterly modern'. Dolan also lauded her 'incredible phrasing – the way she can infuse any line with nuance and power', which he felt served as 'more proof that she's among the greatest interpreters of romantic lyrics'.

Leah Greenblatt, for *Entertainment Weekly*, described 25 as 'a record that feels both new and familiar – a beautiful if safe collection of panoramic ballads and prettily executed detours', while *Billboard* said that Adele's vocal performance was 'swathed in echo, sounding like she's wailing beneath the vaults of the planet's most cavernous cathedral, they hit hard'. *The Times* noted that 'to say a lot is riding on Adele's third album is like saying Elton John likes Christmas'. The reviewer said that 25 'offers few surprises – Adele was never going to take a detour into heavy metal – but plenty of big emotional ballads'. However, he concluded that the album was one of 'great confidence, little arrogance and much charm'.

Negative reviews were few and far between. A regular theme of those was the observation that Adele had not broken much new ground. However, Andy Gill of the *Independent* was less than enthusiastic. He said there were only 'isolated moments of musical intrigue scattered here and there', citing 'River Lea' and 'Send My Love (To Your New Lover)'. However, he added, 'as 25 continues, it's gradually swamped by the kind of dreary piano ballads that are Adele's fall-back position, which leaves things sounding a little too much like they had been designed by committee'.

Alexis Petridis of the *Guardian* said that, in a sense, a review of 25 was 'curiously irrelevant' because 'it has already been taken as read that 25 is a masterpiece: its quality isn't up for question'. But, he said, 'something was missing' from the songs. He also accused Adele of 'going on a bit' – an accusation men often throw at women who express their emotions, and one that Petridis would reprise when he tackled 30. 'Clearly no one buys an Adele album expecting bleeding-edge sonic innovation,' he conceded, 'but the feeling that it doesn't all have to be quite as rounded-edged as this is hard to shake.'

Caroline Framke, for the Vox website, said 25 was Adele's 'least interesting album yet'. She complained that 25 is 'so focused on serving up heavy helpings of Adele's gigantic voice that it rarely goes anywhere new – or even particularly interesting', concluding that 'the album might move you, but it will rarely surprise you'. Across the pond for *The New York Times*, Jon Caramanica wrote that although 'pop moves and mutates', Adele 'more or less does not'. He said her music is 'like time-lapse photography of a busy street: small parts move, but the structure of the whole picture remains essentially intact'.

The *NME* felt the album was 'bombastic but disappointingly safe'. Reviewer Leonie Cooper wrote: 'this is the sound of someone playing the game so safely they might as well have strapped on shin-pads and a crash helmet'. Cooper found things to admire in the collection but concluded that 'you just can't shake the feeling that the whole thing is just far too safe'. *SPIN* magazine said, 'it's a bit jarring to hear someone who has yet to reach their thirtieth birthday sing, "We both know we ain't kids no more" to a presumably also twenty-something ex-lover and then proceed to gaze back upon her youth as if she were doing so from the window of the world's most elegant retirement home'. Journalist T. Cole Rachel remarked that 'too often the tracks on 25 simply feel like sentiments dressed up as songs' which 'offer the kind of mawkish, overcooked melodrama that one imagines Adele could perform in her sleep'.

Jude Rogers, for The Quietus music website, wrote that, on 25, Adele was like 'a friend who you've helped countless times but who won't listen, who actually enjoys being in a mess, whose sparkle gets dampened – gets drowned – as a consequence'. *Time Out* magazine gave perhaps the most negative notice of all. Awarding her third album just two out of five stars, reviewer Oliver Keens said 'most people will consider 25 a bit dull'.

As we have seen, Adele says that she takes any reviews she reads with a pinch of salt. Like most people, she does not enjoy people being negative about her work, but she is self-aware enough to recognize that she, too, has spoken harshly of others, so it would be wrong of her to get too upset. Nevertheless, the real verdict she was awaiting when it came to 25 was that of the record-buying public – how many copies would they buy? Anticipating the sales, she said she did not expect a repeat of 21 sales for 25. 'It was phenomenal what happened, but it was a phenomenon,' she told the BBC.

To say the release was an event is an understatement. The *Independent* said the release might have done nothing less than 'saved the record industry', adding that 25 'sent casual purchasers back to the remaining physical stores and may even have introduced a new generation to the delights of ownership'. In the UK, 25 debuted at Number One on the UK Albums Chart and sold 800,307 copies in its first chart week. This meant it overtook Oasis's third album, *Be Here Now*, to become the fastest-selling album of all time in the UK. As ever, there is a chapter's worth of staggering statistics about the sale of 25, but some stand out as particularly significant. In its first week, 25 sold more copies in the UK than the combined sales of the previous nineteen Number One albums in the UK on their debut week. The album has spent thirteen non-consecutive weeks at Number One in the UK.

Over in the US, the album's first-day sales were 1.49 million, averaging at 62,000 copies per hour, and 1,000 copies per minute. It sold more copies in its first week than any album sold in an entire calendar year in three recent years (2008, 2009 and 2013). Meanwhile, in Europe, 25 also opened at the top of the German charts after selling 263,000 units, the largest weekly sale for a record since 2007. In France, 25 became the fastest-selling album of 2015 after it sold 169,693 copies, of which 26,295 were downloads. It was the world's best-selling album of the year for 2015, with 18.4 million copies sold within the year, and had sold over 29 million copies worldwide by early 2022.

A survey by the business insight company Nielsen, undertaken in December 2015 shortly after 25 was released in America, shone a light on just who was buying her records. It found that a significant percentage of the 'early adopters' buying the physical product of 25 were empty nesters aged fifty-five to sixty-four and most likely from high-income households. Noel Gallagher, the ever-opinionated former Oasis guitarist, might have smiled if he learned that fact. He had, after all, once claimed that Adele's music was for 'f**king grannies'.

This was not to say that the sales of 25 – whether to 'f**king grannies' or otherwise – magically swept away any issues the record industry was suffering from. *Billboard* reported that in 2015, overall album sales both digital and physical experienced a six per cent decline compared to 2014. Adele's third album could only ease that trend: if it was not for the success of 25, the six per cent drop would have been nine per cent: her album made up just over three per cent of the entire total album sales of 2015. Nevertheless, she broke a fifteen-year record when Columbia Records shipped 3.6 million physical copies of 25 across the US, making it the most CDs shipped for a new release since the shipment of 2.4 million copies of NSYNC's 'No Strings Attached' in 2000.

A source in the record industry said that major artists had changed their release dates because they felt they had no hope of competing with 25. 'The major labels have realized it's essential they get out any big releases before then because from November 20, it's very likely to be about one woman only. She will dominate pre-Christmas sales,' the source said. 'That's why Justin Bieber, Kylie Minogue and One Direction are going head-to-head the week before – usually the record companies would want a Number One album with artists that big, but in this case they simply want to get the album out there before Adele.'

Meanwhile, Adele felt that on a personal level she had laid some of the past to rest with 25. 'I think the album is about trying to clear out the past,' she told *i-D*. Having done so, she could move forward. First, though, there was the small matter of awards to be dealt with. At the 2016 BRITs, Adele was Queen of the BRITs again, winning four prizes including best British Female Solo Artist and Best Album. 'To come back after so long away and be so warmly received means so much,' she said. Pundits pointed out she had equalled a record set by Blur, who won the same number in 1995. Take that, Damon Albarn. Her third album fared quite well on some end-of-year lists. *Rolling Stone* magazine and US newspaper *Newsday* ranked the album at Number Two on their 50 Best Albums of 2015 lists, while *Entertainment Weekly* listed the album at Number Three.

Then it was time for her to tour the album. It was her third major concert tour, and took in Western Europe, North America and Oceania during 2016 and 2017. There was a huge demand for tickets. The European headlining dates were announced on 26 November 2015 and went on sale a week later. Many venues reported very swift sell-outs. For instance, the promoters for the Glasgow date reported that tickets for their 13,000-capacity venue sold out within two minutes.

Within weeks Adele then announced the North American leg of the tour, which included six nights at Madison Square Garden in New York City and eight nights at Staples Center in Los Angeles. Ten million people tried to buy tickets to the North American leg of Adele's world tour, but most were disappointed: only 750,000 tickets were available. Nevertheless, this meant Adele broke Taylor Swift's five-show record for most consecutive sold-out shows at Staples Center. Outside one show at that venue, the fans competed with each other to praise Adele. 'She's the first artist we really wanted to see in concert,' said one. 'We don't want to see anyone else.' Another said 'She's real, honest, heartfelt. We're gonna breathe her oxygen. I want to savour it and put it in a jar. ... I sound crazy.'

The tour's Australian leg was announced on 15 November 2016. She booked stadium concerts in five big cities during February and March the following year. Again, the tickets flew out of the door. For instance, her first two shows in New Zealand sold out in a record-breaking twenty-three minutes, and a third show was then announced, with all tickets sold in under thirty minutes. It was in Australia that Adele performed to her largest audience on tour, both in terms of the number of people in the audience for a single show, as well as the overall figure for one city. These records were achieved at Sydney's ANZ Stadium, where her two concerts drew 95,544 people at each show – breaking Taylor Swift's 2015 record of 75,980 audience members at the same venue. The shows were so packed that they caused a huge amount of chaos to the city's public transport system.

The tour enjoyed a triumphant start in Belfast, when Adele told the audience, 'I know some of you have been dragged along here tonight but I'm going to win you over.' It was clear at the end of the show that she had managed that. Her setlist began, appropriately, with 'Hello' before continuing with her first album's 'Hometown Glory'. She then moved effortlessly around her tracks, old and new. The double whammy of 'Someone Like You' and 'Set Fire to the Rain', which she delivered at the end of the main set, could hardly be more powerful. She then re-emerged for the encore with 'All I Ask' and 'When We Were Young', before closing the show with a raucous rendition of 'Rolling in the Deep'. Her audiences would end up on their feet as one, singing along in ecstasy.

Reviewing the opening show in Belfast, Bernadette McNulty of the *Daily Telegraph* wrote that 'Adele undoubtedly has the popularity to fill endless arenas, but maintaining the attention of thousands of people used to the hi-tech extravaganzas laid on by the likes of Taylor Swift and Beyoncé can demand more flashing lights, dance routines and hydraulics than any natural talent.' She added that Adele's entrance was 'certainly theatrical, emerging from the centre of the arena underneath a main stage flanked by an Orwellian projection of her giant eyes blinking' but that Adele 'kept it remarkably and effectively simple, letting nothing get in the way of what was almost a religious communion with her fans'. The BBC's Mark Savage agreed, reporting that 'Adele enjoyed a rapturous reception as she opened her world tour with an intimate arena show in Belfast.'

Reviewing one of Adele's London shows, the *Huffington Post*'s Ashley Percival wrote that 'every single person in the room was in complete awe', while David Smyth from the *Evening Standard* said that 'Adele shifted constantly from being a lightning rod for emotion to a light entertainer.' Meanwhile, the *Financial Times* praised her 'old-school air of professionalism'. At one of the London shows, at the capital's O2 Arena, Adele announced that she would be headlining the Glastonbury Festival in 2016, on 25 June.

She became the fourth solo female to perform a headline set at the festival, and the first on a Saturday.

When the tour reached America, some critics there complained that she spoke too much between the songs, but *Billboard*'s Chris Willman disagreed, writing that 'her actual fans' recognized that they were 'in the presence of not just one of the great singers in pop history, but one of the great broads'. In Australia, Simon Collins of *The West Australian* newspaper concluded that 'for many people, Adele's first ever Australian show and first ever stadium concert will be the best they have ever seen'. He described Adele as a 'once-in-a-generation artist' with a 'unique, yet down-to-earth personality'.

Her set for the Glastonbury Festival was tweaked a little to make it more accessible to a broader audience. Here, the encore closed with 'Someone Like You'. By the time of the 2017 tour dates, the eighteen-track setlist had evolved, but whichever songs she choose, and whatever order she sang them in, Adele had audiences in the palm of her hand. The world felt increasingly divided during these years, and yet Adele's voice could bring people together. However, the tour did end on a disappointing note when Adele was forced to cancel the final two shows, as she had damaged her vocal cords. 'On medical advice I simply am unable to perform over the weekend,' she wrote in an emotional Facebook post. 'To say I'm heartbroken would be a complete understatement.' These cancellations would take on extra significance in 2022, when the Vegas controversy erupted around her.

Concert cancellations inevitably prompt suspicions in some that the act has become a diva, but Adele's down-to-earth personality was in evidence back home in 2017 when she attended a vigil in west London for the victims of the Grenfell Tower fire. On 14 June 2017, a fire broke out high in the twenty-four-storey Grenfell Tower block of flats in Kensington, west London. Seventy-two people died, including two who passed away later in hospital. More than seventy others were injured and 223 people escaped in the deadliest structural fire in the UK since the 1988 Piper Alpha oil-platform disaster. It was also the worst UK residential fire since the Second World War.

The tragedy shook many people, leading to them visiting the site to pay their respects and express their outrage over the lack of protection that the building had offered residents. The day after the fire, as the building was still burning, Adele was seen near the tower, comforting locals. A witness said she was 'going around and hugging everyone she could to comfort them'. According to those present, Adele kept a low profile throughout her visit and was only spotted by a small number of fans.

Just four days later, she surprised firefighters at Chelsea Fire Station by turning up at their station with cakes to thank them for their efforts at Grenfell Tower. It was only when the firefighters opened the door to this unexpected woman in sunglasses that she revealed her identity. Ben King, the station manager, said: 'She just turned up at the station and knocked on the window and said she has some cakes for us. So we opened the door to her and then she took her sunglasses off and said, "Hi, I'm Adele". Everyone was so shocked.' He added that 'she came in, came up to the mess and had a cup of tea with the watch and then she joined us for the minute's silence'.

Weeks later the tragedy was still on her mind. Adele paid tribute to the victims of the Grenfell Tower at one of her Wembley Stadium concerts. She said Wembley's prices for refreshments were 'extortionate' and asked the crowd to donate to victims of the blaze rather than waste their money on 'overpriced wine'.

'It's been two weeks since the fire, and still the people who were affected by it are homeless,' Adele said in a video message before the show. 'I promise that the money we raise together will go directly to the people who are living in that block.' Later, during the show itself, she returned to the theme. 'Usually I ask everyone to get their phone out and put their lights on, but before I do that I want you to donate,' she said.

'Did anyone see the video before I came on? I've been down to Grenfell Tower. I can't tell you how out of control and how chaotic it still is down there, it's been two weeks since this happened ... it's atrocious that we can't get answers.' She added: 'It's our job as human beings to be compassionate ... You'll be hearing a lot more from me about [Grenfell] in the days and weeks and probably years to come.' However, Adele's appeal did not derail the rest of the performance. As the BBC's entertainment reporter, Alex Stanger, observed: 'To be able to talk about something so horrific, but then pick her audience back up again to enjoy the rest of the show, proved Adele's deft hand at performing.'

The way she raised funds – and consciousness – over the Grenfell disaster was a counterpoint to her previous comments about taxation. Speaking to _Q_ magazine in 2011, she had complained about her tax bracket, saying, 'I'm mortified to have to pay fifty per cent!' Warming to her theme, she continued: 'While I use the NHS, I can't use public transport any more. Trains are always late, most state schools are shit, and I've gotta give you, like, four million quid – are you having a laugh? When I got my tax bill in from _19_, I was ready to go and buy a gun and randomly open fire.'

This comment drew a lot of criticism. 'It's hard to feel much sympathy,' said the _Guardian_'s Rob Fitzpatrick, adding that he found it 'upsetting to hear this musician I admire seems as greedy as the most moat-friendly, port-stained Tory grandee'. The *Daily Express* described it as a 'shocking comment' and the *Daily Mail* reported that Adele's words had sparked an 'online backlash'. The *Mirror* said the singer's 'tax moans' would 'strike a wrong note with her fans'. However, there was a note of sympathy five years later, when the BBC noted that she had paid £4 million in UK taxes in the previous year. 'Yep, that puts her in the same tax league as social media giant Facebook,' said the Beeb's website.

Her efforts for the victims of the Grenfell disaster were not the first time Adele had used her talent and fame to help those in need. Throughout her career she has supported causes. As far back as 2007, she was performing at the Little Noise Sessions held at London's Union Chapel, with proceeds from the concerts donated to Mencap, which works with people with learning disabilities. In July and November 2008, Adele performed at the Keep a Child Alive Black Ball on both sides of the Atlantic – the concerts were held in London and New York City respectively. The charity provides healthcare, housing and other support services to HIV- and AIDS-affected communities in Africa and India.

She took part in other fundraising concerts in the US: in September 2009, she performed at the Brooklyn Academy of Music for the VH1 Divas event, a concert to raise money for the Save The Music Foundation charity. Then in December, she opened with a forty-minute set at the second Annual John Mayer Holiday Charity Revue held at the Nokia Theatre in Los Angeles.

ABOVE: Adele won an astonishing six GRAMMY awards that night in 2012, including Record of the Year, Album of the Year, Song of the Year and Best Solo Pop Performance.

RIGHT: With Beyoncé in Los Angeles in 2013. Having admired the singer from her early days, Adele freely admits that Beyoncé continues to be a huge part of her life as an artist.

ABOVE: Backstage at the Oscars in Hollywood in February 2013, posing with actor Richard Gere, after Paul Epworth (left) and Adele picked up the Oscar for 'Skyfall'.

BELOW: In 2013 'Miss Adele Adkins' was awarded an MBE for services to music by the Prince of Wales at an investiture ceremony at Buckingham Palace. A very proud moment.

LEFT: Back to the BRITs in 2016 where Adele collected the Best Solo Artist Award.

MIDDLE: Performing on the Pyramid Stage at Glastonbury in June 2016.

RIGHT: Seen here in Adelaide, Adele played stadium concerts in five major Australian cities during February and March 2017 and enjoyed record-breaking audiences.

Golden Girl: Performing 'I Drink Wine' at the BRITs in 2022, Adele also strolled away with three of the coveted awards.

Adele has largely stayed out of politics, but occasionally her views have been aired. In 2011, Adele called the Conservative prime minister David Cameron 'a wally', and described herself as a 'Labour girl through and through'. She also felt she had to speak out in 2016, when Donald Trump was running for the White House. During his campaign, he used Adele's hits 'Rolling in the Deep' and 'Skyfall' at his political rallies. A fan tweeted that she was 'offended on Adele's behalf', while another asked, 'Does Adele know that Donald Trump plays her songs at his rallies? I have a feeling she would not be pleased.' Trump had previously upset many Adele fans when he jumped the queue at a concert she gave at the Radio City Music Hall. With the divisive Trump now using her songs at rallies, Adele drew a line in the sand. 'Adele has not given permission for her music to be used for any political campaigning,' her spokesman said.

Also, at the 2016 BRIT Awards, she spoke out publicly in support of Kesha, the rap artist who had accused her producer of drugging and sexually assaulting her. Adele has also been an ally to the LGBT community, once dedicating an entire show in Antwerp to victims of the gay nightclub massacre in Orlando.

Two causes seem to have struck a particular chord for Adele. She has been a significant contributor to MusiCares, a charity founded by the National Academy of Recording Arts and Sciences for musicians in need. In 2009, she performed at the MusiCares charity concert in Los Angeles. Then, in 2011 and 2012, she donated autographed items for auctions to raise funds for MusiCares. Given the enormous wealth she has enjoyed from her musical ventures, she wanted to give something back to musicians less fortunate than her.

During her 2011 tour, Adele required all backstage visitors and guests receiving complimentary tickets to the North American dates to donate a minimum charitable contribution of $20 to the UK charity Sands, which is dedicated to 'supporting anyone affected by the death of a baby and promoting research to reduce the loss of babies' lives'. Guests were asked to make this donation when they collected their tickets from the box office. There was no choice in this matter: 'There will be no exception to this rule,' her rider document noted. She had insisted on a similar rule during the European leg of her 2011 tour, raising nearly £10,000 during that part of the tour alone. Adele has never spoken about whether her support for the Sands cause was the result of something she had personally been affected by, but her action certainly raised plenty of praise for her. Like many people, some of her charitable activity has been influenced directly by personal experiences. For instance, she has given monthly donations to Great Ormond Street Hospital in London because of the care they gave to one of her cousins, who suffered from acute epilepsy. *Cosmopolitan* magazine led a chorus of praise for this move. 'What a great idea!' they said. 'We'd love to see more celebs doing that.'

Elsewhere in her tour material, Adele required promoters to provide her with a pack of Marlboro Lights cigarettes and a disposable lighter, a selection of chewing gum, and a small plate of 'freshly made, individually wrapped sandwiches' that 'must NOT contain tomatoes, vinegar, chilli or citrus fruit'. For after each concert, Adele asked that her tour bus be stocked with a selection of 'bite-size' chocolate bars, including Twix, Aero, Milky Way, and Mars. She also requested organic muesli and six cereal bars. Turning to drinks, her rider stated that Adele required two bottles of the 'very best quality red wine' and twelve bottles of 'best quality European lager beer, i.e. Becks, Stella Artois, Peroni, etc.' The note also added, somewhat thunderingly: 'North American beer is NOT acceptable.'

CHAPTER SEVEN

MARRIED NOW

As we have seen, Adele can be most minimalist when it comes to announcements about her personal life. For instance, when she gave birth in October 2012 there was no announcement as such. The only statement from the communications agency Purple PR was a statement saying they were 'not releasing a statement'. To celebrate the birth, Konecki bought Adele a £3,000 gold pendant, designed by a friend. He wore a matching one himself.

Their son's name was not revealed initially. Adele made her first public appearance since her pregnancy at the Golden Globe Awards in 2013. She confirmed that she had given birth to a son and that she planned to keep his name private, calling it 'personal'. A few days later, she revealed that she nicknamed him 'Little Peanut', or simply 'Peanut' for short. It was not until December 2014, after waves of feverish speculation, that Adele confirmed the child's name to be Angelo through a note to Elton John that was posted online. The cat had rather left the bag anyway when she had been seen leaving a Hollywood store wearing a gold necklace bearing the name 'Angelo'.

After that, the next area of public fascination was over whether, and when, she and Konecki would marry. The couple celebrated their five-year anniversary on 17 October 2016. That evening, Konecki surprised Adele during her concert in Nashville by replacing some of the usual white confetti that would rain down during the show with pink confetti covered with handwritten notes to her. The rumour about their marriage gathered pace when she was spotted out and about in Beverly Hills in early 2017. Adele's casual outfit couldn't have been less remarkable. She wore a black sweater, a long tie-dye dress, a pair of sunglasses and a black fedora. So far, so casual. A typical day out for our understated heroine, who has rarely felt the need to do herself up to the nines every time she leaves her front door.

However, it was the gold ring on her ring finger that really got the tongues wagging. Was this proof that Adele and Simon Konecki had tied the knot? Naturally, people quickly put two and two together, because Konecki had been spotted with a similar gold band on his finger while out in Los Angeles with Angelo the previous day. The Adele marriage whirlwind was officially underway and there would be no stopping it.

Marriage rumours about celebrities are part of the stock-in-trade of the media. They are a huge preoccupation for journalists – second only in their obsession with divorce. But before the media can go hunting for signs that a celebrity's marriage is on the rocks, that marriage has to take place. With Adele, a celebrity who combines enormous popularity with a commitment to retain privacy, the race to find the first clue that she was married was a breathless one.

The month after her ring raised curiosity, Adele as good as confirmed the rumours while picking up another of her gongs. During her acceptance speech for Album of the Year at the GRAMMYs, she said: 'GRAMMYs, I appreciate it. The Academy, I love you. My manager, my husband and my son – you're the only reason I do it.' If this felt like clear confirmation at last, Adele muddied the waters later that same night as her teasing continued. Shortly after the show, she switched the terminology and referred to Konecki as her 'partner', rather than 'husband'. Curiouser and curiouser: she certainly seemed to be toying with us. As we shall see, this was exactly what she was doing.

As the speculation about her wedding grew, the media was naturally desperate to put some flesh on the bones. *Heat* magazine thought that Adele had organized a small ceremony, with just 'family and close friends' invited. The report claimed she and Simon married at their £10-million home in Los Angeles without any 'fuss'. It wasn't until March 2017 that Adele settled the issue. She was on stage in Brisbane, Australia, referring to her track 'Someone Like You', when she seemingly cleared up the matter. Describing the moment that she first played 'Someone Like You' to family and friends, she said, 'I could see in their eyes as they were listening to it on their headphones that it reminded them of something or someone.' She added that 'as bad as a break up can be, as bitter and horrible and messy as it can be, that feeling when you first fall for someone is the best feeling on earth, and I am addicted to that feeling', adding: 'Obviously I can't go through with those feelings because I'm married now. I've found my next person.'

There we had it – Adele had finally clarified it. Or had she? In 2021 she revealed that 'the timeline the press have of my relationship, my marriage, is actually completely wrong'. During an interview with *Vogue* magazine, she said, 'We got married when I was thirty … and then I left.' Asked by the interviewer how soon after their marriage she and Konecki split up, she said, 'I'm not gonna go into that detail, remember I am embarrassed. This is very embarrassing.' However, she said of her marriage that 'it wasn't very long'.

So, why had she referred to him as her husband prior to their marriage? 'I always called him my husband, because we had a kid together,' she explained in the same interview. Was it that, or was it more that she liked playing with the media. 'They know nothing!' she cackled. 'I've got the upper hand on everything. I love it.'

However, her divorce would be no laughing matter. 'So, when I was thirty, my entire life fell apart and I had no warning of it,' she said, summing up the experience. Adele was naturally heartbroken when her marriage came apart. She also felt another strong emotion – embarrassment. 'Having so many people that I don't know *know* that I didn't make the marriage work … It f***ing devastated me,' said

Adele, during an interview with *Rolling Stone* magazine. 'I was embarrassed.'

The intense difficulty Adele felt over her divorce had its roots in her earliest years and the pain of her parents' break-up. This pain led her to want what she was denied: a grounded and traditional family unit. She wanted for her child what she had lost after her father left home when she was just two years old. 'I've been obsessed with a nuclear family my whole life because I never came from one,' she told Oprah Winfrey. 'From a very young age [I] promised myself that, when I had kids, we'd stay together,' she said, adding, 'And I tried for a really, really long time.'

She first noticed that all was not well with her marriage when she took a personality test in a women's magazine, as she explained to Winfrey. 'One of the questions asked, "What's something that no one would ever know about you?"', and she suddenly told her friends, 'I'm really not happy. I'm not living, I'm just plodding along.' Their reaction was one of surprise. 'They all gasped,' she recalled. 'From there, I was like "What am I doing? What am I doing it for?"'

Legal documents were lodged at a court in Los Angeles, but the former couple decided to keep their break-up as low key as possible. For some celebrities, the temptation to make a huge media event of their divorce is irresistible. They leak details to the tabloids, grant an exclusive interview to a celebrity weekly magazine in which they break down theatrically, and then eventually sign a book deal. It's an undignified path but one that is very well trodden nonetheless

– and it can pay very well in the twin celebrity currencies of cash and attention.

However, Adele is a different kind of star – one who walks with dignity rather than desperation – so she wanted to handle the divorce with as much class and compassion as possible. She didn't speak of it publicly until three years had passed because she wanted to protect Angelo and avoid a circus of eternal speculation. 'We kept it to ourselves for a very long time,' she said of the break-up. 'We had to take our time because there was a child involved. It would always be like, "Where's Adele? Oh, she's working," or, "Where's Simon? He's in England."'

The initial legal filing showed that both parties asked for joint custody and visitation of their son, which they planned to negotiate through a mediator. In March 2020, they signed a confidentiality agreement in regard to the details of the case. The divorce was officially signed off by a judge in March 2021. 'It was overdue,' said Adele of the divorce.

While her consideration for Angelo undoubtedly influenced her approach to the divorce, perhaps her self-confessed embarrassment at how quickly the marriage failed also stopped her from rushing to announce it. She told *Vogue* she is 'fully aware' of the irony of her being 'the heartbreak girl who found her person' and then 'f**ked up' because the marriage 'didn't work'. She told Heart radio that although the divorce was 'exhausting' and 'really hard work' she recognizes that she 'was able to take the time that I needed, which isn't a given for everyone'. Adele added that 'the more and more you put it off, the worse and worse it gets', admitting that she 'had been putting it off anyway for years before'.

Nevertheless, she said she is still close to Konecki and is glad that she had her first child with him. 'I definitely chose the perfect person to have my child with,' she said: 'that – after making a lot of knee-jerk reactions – is one of my proudest things I've ever done.' She added of her ex-husband: 'I'd trust him with my life.' Following their split, Konecki lived across the road from Adele in a house she bought for him. They share custody and hold regular family movie nights.

'Angelo couldn't have a better dad,' she told *The Face*. 'Simon is so invested and so interested. He gets onto his level in anything. Whatever Angelo is into, what he wants to watch, where he wants to go and play, his new fucking playground games that change every week – he is a big child in that sense of being so curious with him.'

Indeed, when the split was officially announced by Adele's representatives, Angelo was at the heart of the statement. 'They are committed to raising their son together lovingly,' the announcement said. 'As always they ask for privacy. There will be no further comment.'

She later told *Vogue* that an upside of the divorce was that it meant she went through the soul-searching that many experienced during the Covid-19 pandemic a year earlier. 'Everyone had to face a lot of their demons, because they had so much time on their hands with nothing to distract them,' she said. 'They had to face themselves in isolation. Whereas I did that the year before.'

More reflection on what had happened gave her a greater perspective on what went wrong.' I was just going through the motions and I wasn't happy,' she told *Vogue*. 'Neither of us did anything wrong. Neither of us hurt each other or anything like that. It was just: I want my son to see me really love, and be loved. It's really important to me.' She went into therapy and put herself through quite the process. 'Well, my therapist told me that I had to sit with my little seven-year-old self,' she told *Vogue*. 'Because she was left on her own. And I needed to go sit with her and really address how I felt when I was growing up. And issues with my dad. Which I'd been avoiding.'

She learned what those issues had meant for her. 'Not being sure if someone who is supposed to love you loves you, and doesn't prioritize you in any capacity when you're little,' she said. 'You assume it and get used to it. So my relationship with men in general, my entire life, has always been: "You're going to hurt me, so I'll hurt you first." It's just toxic and prevents me from actually finding any happiness. Sometimes, with my own son, he could talk to me in a certain way, and I shut down. With my own fucking child. I'll take it so to heart, what he's saying, when actually what he's saying is, No, I don't want to go to bed.' Therefore, in her romantic relationships with men, she would expect things not to work out. 'And being okay with it, because you had to be okay with it when you were younger.'

She embarked on what has been described to *Vogue* as her 'year of anxiety'. From her 'Early Life Crisis' to a 'year of anxiety', Adele was good at giving names to her trials. 'It was a lot of sound baths. It was a lot of meditation. It was a lot of therapy. And a lot of time spent on my own,' she said. She grew to enjoy working out in the gym because 'it became my time', she said. She worked on her lower back and stomach areas, but it was a more holistic project than that. 'I realized that when I was working out, I didn't have any anxiety. It was never about losing weight. I thought, if I can make my body physically strong, and I can feel that and see that, then maybe one day I can make my emotions and my mind physically strong.'

Adele's weight has been an obsession for the media. 'The press are always trying to bring it up,' she had told the *Daily Telegraph*, 'but I really don't give a toss. If I wanted to be on the cover of *FHM*, then of course I'd be, like, f***, I need to lose weight or, I need some fake tan or I need to get my teeth fixed. But I'd rather be on the cover of *Q* for my music.'

Nevertheless, she did lose a lot of weight and become generally more physically and emotionally healthy. 'I'm definitely really happy now,' she said. 'I'm more agile because I can now move more, because of my back. I got my core strong. I slipped my first disc when I was fifteen from sneezing. I was in bed and I sneezed and my fifth one flew out. In January, I slipped my sixth one, my L6. And then where I had a C-section, my core was useless.' That said, the rebuilding of her confidence was not a fast project. She said she would enjoy a 'lovely night with my friends' but then 'wake up like a tsunami was coming for me'. She remembers sitting with two friends and asking, 'When will I stop feeling like this?' They told her she would feel better in time. 'And I was like, yeah, but how much time? And one of them cried and was just like, "I don't know. It's gonna be a ride." And it was.'

She made friends with a woman in Los Angeles who was in her forties. Adele would meet her new friend and unload her experiences and feelings. 'She would be like, mmm hmm,' remembered Adele. 'She'd be like, yeah, that happened to me once. I felt like that once. I'd be there having these meltdowns. Like, sobbing, sobbing, sobbing. And she'd be so calm.' The tattoo of a mountain on Adele's right wrist seems to have been inspired by these exchanges. 'I told my friend, I feel like I'm on a steep mountain, trying to get up to the top,' Adele told Oprah. 'And she was like, you will get there. And you'll have a nice leisurely stroll down. And then there'll be another fucking mountain. And I'm like, I'm not even over this one yet. And she was like, that's just life.'

Part of Adele's life following the divorce was squaring what had happened with her son. There were challenging moments, including a disturbing question he asked her when he was just six and a half years old. 'He said to my face, "Can you see me?" And I was like, "Uh, yeah." And he was like, "'Cause I can't see you,"' she said. 'Well, my whole life fell apart in that moment. He knew I wasn't there.'

It was after that conversation that she began conversing more intimately with Angelo. However, she found he had 'so many simple questions for me that I can't answer, because I don't know the answer'. For instance, she told *Rolling Stone*, he asked why the family couldn't still live together. 'That's just not what people do when they get divorced,' she replied.

'But why not?' he pressed. 'I'm like, I don't fucking know. That's not what society does.' He also asked why she didn't love his father anymore. 'And I'd be like, I do love your dad. I'm just not in love. I can't make that make sense to a nine year old.' She added, 'If I can reach the reason why I left, which was the pursuit of my own happiness, even though it made Angelo really unhappy – if I can find that happiness and he sees me in that happiness, then maybe I'll be able to forgive myself for it.'

Adele is open about how much motherhood changed her. She has been honest about the sacrifices Penny made for her, and, accordingly, she is straightforward about what she has given up for Angelo. Materially, the multi-millionaire, West Coast-dwelling Adele's sacrifices are different to those Penny made when she was struggling in Finsbury Park and Tottenham, but the fact of sacrifice remains and Adele is unabashed at pointing this out, even from her position of comparative privilege.

'There are definitely a few elements of myself that I don't think I'll ever get back,' she told *The Face*. 'More than anything, it's the freedom of being able to do whatever you want, whenever you want. Going somewhere and not having to prioritize someone else.' She added that 'giving, giving, giving, to a baby or a toddler, when they can't even fucking talk to you, your brain goes a bit mushy' because 'you're not stimulated very much'. She also suffered from 'really quite bad' postpartum depression. She remembered 'having no time to even brush my teeth, let alone write a record or hang out with my friends'. Her 'friends … hobbies, the things I like doing without a baby, are things that make me who I am' but she 'didn't really have access to that for a while'. She found it easier as the years went by. 'When they get older – he is so funny! He's brilliant. He's a fucking comedian, like an actual comedian,' she said. 'It's way easier to navigate once you can really communicate with them. He's about to turn nine and he's getting to the point now where he's got opinions. It's fucking fun!'

When she lost weight, it made headlines. Whether she is large, small or anywhere in between, it seems that Adele's size will always be worth column inches to the media. 'My body's been objectified my entire career,' she told *Glamour* online magazine. 'It's not just now.' She understood why the dramatic weight loss was 'a shock' for lots of people. 'I understand why some women especially were hurt. Visually I represented a lot of women,' she said, 'but I'm still the same person.' This gave her cause to reflect that 'the most brutal conversations were being had by other women about my body'. She said she was 'very fucking disappointed with that' because it hurt her feelings.

That was not the end of the story, though. As ever with Adele, anyone who really wants to know what is going on in her life can look beyond interviews and public statements. For the answers to some questions lie in her music. Both in her lyrics and the mood of the tracks, she lays herself bare. 'Easy on Me' was the first track the world heard from her album 30, and it covered her feelings about the divorce. Even the video was themed around her heartbreak. She takes a final look around an empty house, climbs into her car and drives off, passing a 'Sold' sign. She sings: 'Go easy on me, baby.' She pleads that 'You can't deny how hard I tried, I changed who I was to put you both first but now I give up.'

She expanded on the link during an interview on the Hits Radio Breakfast Show. 'The whole album is sort of dedicated to my son more than anything, but, yeah, it's about my relationship with his dad and with him,' she said. 'It's like you could be in, you know, discussion or disagreement or a full-blown row if you want, not that me and his dad ever used to do that.'

She continued: 'If you're the one that's sort of initiating the discussion, it'd sort of be like, "Well hang on a minute, go easy on me, you know, it's not my fault." So it's just sort of really about that in the way that, you know, the decision that I made really, so yeah.' Speaking to *Vogue*, she expanded more about the meaning of the track. 'It's not like anyone's having a go at me,' she said, 'but it's like, I left the marriage. Be kind to me as well. It was the first song I wrote for the album and then I didn't write anything else for six months after because I was like, "OK, well, I've said it all."'

In the same interview, she spoke about how her marriage ended, agreeing that it ended more with 'drift' than 'implosion'. 'Yeah,' she said. 'It just wasn't … It just wasn't right for me anymore. I didn't want to end up like a lot of other people I knew. I wasn't *miserable* miserable, but I would have been miserable had I not put myself first. But, yeah, nothing bad happened or anything like that.' She admitted that she would sometimes wake up in the morning with a feeling of 'anxiety' because she couldn't remember what she had or had not said to Angelo about the separation. So her then therapist suggested she record voice notes of their conversations so she wouldn't wake up scared in the mornings, wondering what she'd said to her son. Some of these would be shared with the public, in a move that surprised many.

However, she insisted, there was never any tension between her and Konecki over access to their son. 'Obviously Simon and I never fought over him or anything like that,' she told *Vogue*. 'Angelo's just like, "I don't get it."' She added, 'I don't really get it either. There are rules that are made up in society of what happens and doesn't happen in marriage and after marriage, but I'm a very complex person. I've always let him know how I'm feeling from a very young age because I felt quite frazzled as an adult.'

Eventually, she sank to her lowest point, when she was 'terrified' about what was going to happen. 'People were everywhere, trying to get stories, and I just hated it. I was embarrassed. I was really embarrassed. That thing of not being able to make something work. We've been trained as women to keep trying, even by the movies we watched when we were little. At the time it broke my heart, but I actually find it so interesting now. How we're told to suck it up. Well, f**k that.'

During her in-depth interview with Oprah Winfrey in 2021 she expanded on her feeling of shame over the divorce. She said she takes marriage very seriously but realized that, thanks to her quick divorce, it might seem like she did not. 'Almost like I disrespected it by getting married and then divorced so quickly. I'm embarrassed because it was so quick.' She said she wanted her music to help Angelo eventually understand what happened and why. 'I wanted to explain to him through this record, when he's in his twenties or thirties, who I am and why I voluntarily chose to dismantle his entire life in the pursuit of my own happiness,' she said.

Then, when a snippet of another track, 'Hold On', was previewed for the public, the connection with her divorce was immediately apparent. 'I swear to God, I'm such a mess, the harder I try, I regress,' she sang. 'Every day feels like the road I'm on might just open up and swallow me whole.' The lyrics to the song also included 'Let time be patient, let pain be gracious, just hold on.' Asked during a question-and-answer session on Instagram what inspired the new collection, she was clear as a crystal. 'Divorce, babe,' she said. 'Divorce.' *The New Yorker* duly dubbed *30* as Adele's 'divorce album'. Before the album was even released or shared with the media, the publication said it was a 'document of personal trauma and turbulence'. Public fascination was growing.

As she made the album, she realized that her lack of anger towards Konecki was a 'problem'. She told *Vogue*, ''Cause all the other albums are like, You did this! You did that! Fuck you! Why can't you arrive for me? Then I was like: Oh, shit, I'm the running theme, actually. Maybe it's me!' She went as far as insisting that *30* is not a divorce album. 'It was more me divorcing myself,' she said with a laugh. 'Just being like, Bitch, fuckin' hot mess, get your fuckin' shit together!' So, if it was not a divorce album it was still her album – and she hoped to keep it that way. 'I always say that 21 doesn't belong to me anymore, everyone else took it into their hearts so much,' she said. 'I'm not letting go of this one. This is my album. I want to share myself with everyone, but I don't think I'll ever let this one go.' All the same, she is under no illusions that she can wave a magic wand over the pain of a family break-up, especially for her son. 'It made him really unhappy sometimes,' she said. 'And that's a real wound for me that I don't know if I'll ever be able to heal.'

It's worth pausing to note again that not all celebrities handle their divorces with as much dignity as Adele. In some cases, when famous people dissolve their marriages it creates a media frenzy (and epic court battle) that lasts longer than their unions. They have even launched their own buzzwords: 'conscious uncoupling' has become a recent addition to the lexicon which has long featured other more familiar clichés such as 'irreconcilable differences', and pleas for the public to 'respect the privacy' of stars. Sometimes these pleas are somewhat disingenuous.

It takes all sorts: Kim Kardashian's split from basketball player Kris Humphries, her second partnership, took eight times as long as their union, but Tom Cruise and Katie Holmes had a signed settlement eleven days after Holmes filed for divorce. Kim Kardashian and Kris Humphries were married for seventy-two days, Nicolas Cage and Erika Koike's marriage lasted for four days, but Zsa Zsa Gabor and actor Felipe de Alba surpassed them all by being married for one day – 13 April 1983 – before Gabor sought an annulment.

So although Adele is, by her own admission, embarrassed by the swift failure of her marriage, her union was lengthy compared to that of some celebrities, and the way she has handled its ending is a picture of dignity compared with the divorce of many stars. That Adele's music has class has never been in doubt. However, that the woman herself is classy is shown clearly by her divorce. The key takeaway from how Adele handled her divorce is that she managed to keep it under wraps for a year: she separated from Konecki in 2018, but didn't announce the news publicly until 2019. Can you imagine that sort of discretion from Kim Kardashian?

She has never spoken vindictively of Konecki. On the contrary, she credits him with 'saving her life' after she became famous. 'At that time in my life, I was so young and I think I would have got in all of it,' she told Oprah Winfrey. 'I could have easily gone down some dodgy paths and self-destructed from being so overwhelmed by all of it. And he came in and was the most stable person I'd ever had in my life up until that point.'

As is often the case with Adele, for all her eloquence and artistry in her songs, she is also capable of a soundbite that does the job and at the same time makes people chuckle. Looking back over her divorce, she mused, 'I'd say it's worth it, you know treading through all of that poo is worth it.' In the wake of the divorce, Adele noted that a lot of her friends were engaging in casual sex. 'And I was like, I'm not doing that,' she told Zane Lowe on Apple Music 1. 'I'm not, I'm not, that's not … I've left my marriage to go forward, not to f***ing go backwards.'

In the wake of the divorce, she wanted to enjoy some 'me' time. So she holidayed in Anguilla with former One Direction heart-throb Harry Styles and the comedian James Corden. Photos of Styles wearing a Mickey Mouse t-shirt during their break on the glamorous Caribbean island were overshadowed by the photographs of Adele showing a dramatic weight loss. There was also plenty of press excitement when Styles left a huge £1,545 tip after the group dined at a restaurant on New Year's Day.

The trip marked quite a moment for the pair, as they have some history. Nine years earlier, when Harry was just seventeen years old, he said in an interview with Capital FM that he had a crush on Adele and that she made him 'weak at the knees'. When she described him as 'cute' in another interview, he spoke about her again, saying he would love to date the 'incredible' singer.

The following year, during the BRIT Awards, the *Mirror* asked Harry which stars he would like to kiss during the awards party. 'Adele, definitely Adele,' he replied. Soon, they were in touch. Appearing on BBC Radio 1 after he had turned twenty-one, he said, 'For my twenty-first she gave me one of her albums, 21, and said, "I did some pretty cool stuff when I was twenty-one, good luck."'

In 2016, when Harry was working on his single 'Sign of the Times', he said, 'I've spoken to her a little bit, she knows one of the guys that I wrote [his album] with a lot.' But when they actually holidayed together, the rumour mill went into overdrive. According to unnamed sources, Harry was Adele's 'rock' following her split from husband Simon

Konecki. It was also claimed that Harry had introduced Adele to Bulletproof coffee – a black coffee drink mixed with butter and coconut oil that he reportedly uses to curb his appetite. The trip, and her friendship with Styles, helped to ease the pain of her divorce.

However, after already losing one man in her life, she soon lost another. Luckily, in the years before her father's death, the two had made an effort to try and resolve their differences. The death of a loved one that you are close to can hit you hard. They were a part of your life. But the death of a relative from whom you were estranged can hit hard in a different – and often more painful – way. In both cases you have lost someone of significance, but in the latter scenario you are hit by regrets.

When Marc Evans died in 2021, it could have happened with lots of unresolved issues. She has spoken of the impact his exit had on her life. Talking to Oprah Winfrey, she said that the 'biggest wound' she'd suffered as a child was the 'absolute lack of presence and effort' from her father. She added that she had 'absolutely zero expectations of anybody, because I learned not to have them through my dad', explaining that 'he was the reason I haven't fully accessed what it is to be in a loving, loving relationship with somebody'.

He had seemingly blown it when he sold his story to the tabloids in 2011. An interview with the *Sun* appeared under the headline 'I was an alcoholic and a rotten dad to Adele. It tears me up inside.' He was quoted as saying that he was 'deeply ashamed' of what he'd become and felt that 'the kindest thing I could do for Adele was to make sure she never saw me in that state'.

Evans later insisted that he granted this interview thinking that his daughter had cleared his discussion with the journalist. He said that Adele had agreed to give a joint interview with him, so the tabloids would leave him alone. 'Don't worry, Dad, we'll do it together,' he claimed she said. The Welshman said that Adele subsequently pulled out of any such arrangement but he thought she gave him her blessing to do it alone. For Adele, this interview seemed to cross a very painful line. 'He's f***ing blown it,' she said, according to the BBC. 'He'll never hear from me again ... If I ever see him I will spit in his face.'

Perhaps her anger was understandable. Evans had sold a story to the *Sun*, telling them that he felt guilty about not being there for Adele when she was growing up. When a *Rolling Stone* journalist later asked Adele about this episode, the singer's eyes narrowed. 'I never knew my dad,' she says. 'He has no fuckin' right to talk about me.' What made matters worse was that the day after Evans' story was published, another one appeared. As part of the 'research' for the second article, a reporter had ambushed her grandmother at a bus stop for an interview. This shook Adele, who told *Rolling Stone*: 'That's when I started smoking again.'

In 2013, Evans revealed he had bowel cancer and told the media that he was worried he would die before he got to meet his grandson, Angelo, who was then ten months old. 'I still haven't met Angelo and I'm facing the fact I may never do,' the fifty-one-year-old grandfather told the *Daily Mail*.

'It could be over for me before I get to make my peace with Adele.' He added, 'The years are going by and I'm worried I'm not going to see my grandson and do the things with him that I did when Adele was a child.'

It seemed for a moment that the two had settled their differences when Evans subsequently claimed that they rekindled their relationship during the making of Adele's third studio album, 25. He told the *Sun on Sunday*, 'Adele and I are fine, it was a misunderstanding. We've patched things up, everything's fine, but I don't want to make further comment.' However, Adele strongly denied any such reconciliation had taken place. This seemed to be an echo of when he had alleged that he and his daughter had made up and shared a drink a few nights before she had embarked on her Adele Live tour in support of 21. Again, at that time Adele denied his statements.

In 2017, as she accepted the Record of the Year award at the GRAMMYs, she seemingly took a swipe at her father, in the form of a compliment to her manager, Jonathan Dickins. 'Thank you to my manager because the comeback, as it were, was completely masterminded by him,' she began. 'And you executed it incredibly, and I owe you everything. We've been together for ten years, and I love you like you're my dad.' However, she then rather muddied the waters, by saying: 'I love you so, so much. I don't love my dad, that's the thing. That doesn't mean a lot.' To try and clarify the moment, she added, 'I love you like I *would* love my dad.' For Evans, this will have been painful, and it was not the only pain he suffered after speaking to tabloids. One night he was in a local pub and four paratroopers learned of his connection with Adele. 'Yeah, I'm her f***king auntie,' said one of the men.

Later that night, as Evans was walking home, the men pulled up beside him in a car. 'I thought, "Oh no,"' he said. The men then proceeded to 'hit shit out of me', he recalled later. Luckily, two women driving past saw the attack and pulled up. They beeped their horn and asked what the paratroopers were doing. However, Evans was left with an injury to his left eye area and later had to undergo surgery.

So relations between Adele and her father had reached a low point and both of them were, in their different ways, hurting due to the estrangement. However, she has revealed that she did in fact begin to reconcile with Evans around 2018, after he became seriously ill. He admitted to her that he had only ever listened to one of her songs – 'Hometown Glory'. 'He never ever played any of my other music,' she told Winfrey. 'He was like, "It's too painful."' Adele was keen for him to hear more of her material. At the top of the list of tracks she wanted to play him one was of her new songs, 'To Be Loved'. In this track, she has tried to express how her father's absence had affected her ability to trust other people. Unsurprisingly, playing it for him proved to be a powerful experience: 'It was amazing for me and him,' she said. Here, at least, they were able to find common ground on something as father and daughter. 'I think he could listen to me sing it, but not saying it – we are very similar like that,' she added.

There was some comfort for them both in the fact that she managed to play him all of her new album over Zoom, shortly before he died in April 2021. To Adele's amazement, the more of her music that she played for her father, the more common ground they found. 'His favourites were all of my favourites, which was amazing,' she told Winfrey, 'and he was proud of me for doing it. So it was very, very healing [and] when he died, it was literally like the wound closed up.'

These were emotional, if distant, encounters. For many people around the globe, the Covid pandemic forced them to hold powerful, difficult and sometimes harrowing occasions online. Many family members had their last moments through webcams, unable to be together because of lockdown rules. Funerals became 'virtual' affairs, with grieving relatives forced to navigate the settings of Zoom and other software for the chance to watch their lost relative's farewell service.

However, while for some this added to the pain, there is no doubt that the online reconciliation between Adele and her father was soothing for both. Had the world not been opened up to virtual meetings due to the pandemic, would father and daughter necessarily have connected this way in his dying months? As Adele has said, their conversations were 'healing'. So much so, that she said she could feel the wound closing up.

Marc Evans died at the age of fifty-seven, after cancer finally claimed him.

CHAPTER EIGHT

THE WORLD STOPS

By the time the fourth Adele album, *30*, was approaching release, the extravaganza of the build-up to its launch had become a familiar process. Sure enough, for *30*, the guessing game over its release date started early. In February 2020, Adele announced at her friend Laura Dockrill's wedding that the new album would be out in September of that year. However, Covid-19 had other ideas. As it turned out, *30* would not see the light of day until the November of 2021. The period in between was painful for everyone in the world, thanks to the Covid pandemic – as Adele said, 'no one wants to remember this period of time'.

One soundtrack of that period of time was the rumour mill, steadily humming a backdrop of speculation over the much-anticipated fourth album from Adele. The producer of her previous two albums, Paul Epworth, was asked what was going on. 'I don't know, my phone ain't ringing,' he replied. Adele's manager, Jonathan Dickins, had a bit more information. In 2020 he told industry magazine *Music Week*,

'It isn't coming in September, it'll be ready when it's ready.' He added, 'We're all in the same boat, you're doing stuff and then all of a sudden, the world stops. It'll come when it's ready. I can't put a date on that yet. We have music, but we're still working.'

Then Adele was asked directly by a fan when the album might appear. In August 2020, she posted on Instagram about how she'd been reading the blogger and social activist Glennon Doyle's latest book, *Untamed*. She wrote, 'I am so ready for myself after reading this book! It's as if I just flew into my body for the very first time. Whew! Anyone who has any kind of capacity to truly let go and give in to yourself with any kind of desire to hold on for dear life—Do it.'

Adele told her fans that 'This book will shake your brain and make your soul scream.' *Untamed* is certainly an eye-opening, gripping read, right from the off. It charts the dissolution of Doyle's marriage, and how she found love with soccer star Abby Wambach. The book begins with a hooking line: 'Four years ago, married to the father of my three children, I fell in love with a woman.' Adele advised would-be readers that they might like to mark out key passages. 'You'll want to refer back to it trust me!' she wrote.

So high was anticipation for Adele's new album that it was perhaps inevitable that the phrase 'I am so ready for myself' was interpreted by some as a hint that its release was impending. A fan asked her about this underneath Adele's post, commenting: 'Adele, where's the album?' Adele, who is known to respond to fans' comments occasionally, replied: 'I honestly have no idea.' She had been asked in June whether another Instagram post was an album hint. She replied: 'Of course it's not. Corona ain't over. I'm quarantining. Wear a mask and be patient.'

In October 2020, she poked her head back into the public eye when she hosted the US comedy TV show *Saturday Night Live*. She told the viewers that her album was 'not finished'. Referencing her weight loss, she added, 'I know I look really, really different since you last saw me,' as she took to the stage. 'But actually, because of all the Covid restrictions ... I had to travel light and I could only bring half of me – and this is the half I chose.' She added that she was 'too scared' to sing and host *SNL* at the same time. 'I'd rather just put on some wigs, have a glass of wine or six and see what happens,' she said.

During her opening monologue on the programme, Adele said she was 'absolutely thrilled' to be part of the show that 'broke my career in America, twelve long years ago'. She continued, 'You see I was the musical guest back in 2008 when Sarah Palin came on with Tina Fey, so obviously a few million people tuned in to watch it. And well, the rest is now history.' In one memorable scene, she took part in a spoof of the reality show *The Bachelor*. 'I'm here because I've had a lot of heartbreak in my life – first at nineteen and then, sort of famously, at twenty-one and then, even more famously, at twenty-five,' she said. She was repeatedly rejected by potential dates during the sketch but interrupted proceedings with songs – including 'Rolling in the Deep', 'Hello' and 'Set Fire to the Rain'. In other sketches, she played a ghost haunting a mansion, and an English woman who was secretly obsessed with colouring books and having her fortune told.

It was a fun appearance that thrilled her fans. Little had been seen or heard of her for a while, after all. However, it could not satisfy the intense hunger for her new album. The speculation carried on: there were rumours that the American soul singer and producer Raphael Saadiq was working on the album, alongside the crooner John Legend. She spent three years working on the album with top-tier co-writers, notably ubiquitous American pop master Greg Kurstin (who has also worked with Lily Allen, Pink and Lana Del Rey) and in-demand British producer Dean Josiah Cover, a.k.a. Inflo (the mystery man behind acclaimed soul collective SAULT).

As with 25, there was tension behind the scenes between Adele and the money men at her label. In an interview with broadcaster Zane Lowe, she remembered a meeting when someone at her label highlighted the importance of making sure fourteen-year-old teenagers knew who she was. 'I'm like, "But they've all got mums!"' Adele said. 'If everyone's making music for the TikTok, who's making music for my generation, for my peers? I'll do that job gladly. I'd rather cater to people that are on my level in terms of the time we've spent on Earth.' She flatly rejected the idea that twelve-year-old children should even listen to 30. 'It's too deep! Thirty- and forty-year-olds are all committing to themselves and doing therapy. That's my vibe. That's what I was doing.' It seemed as if with every album the money men would attempt to get Adele to sell out her vision, and each time she would send them away with a flea in their ears. It would be her album, not theirs.

She also put her foot down when it came to the size of the team she would hire for the album. In contrast to her previous album, which involved eleven producers, Adele said that for *30* she 'chose a relatively small pool of people' including pop hitmaker Max Martin and his regular collaborator Shellback, as well as Greg Kurstin, Ludwig Göransson and Inflo.

More than with her previous albums, there was the sense that Adele was writing *30* for Adele, as much as for the rest of us. The feeling was that Adele wanted to wrestle back something she felt she had lost in becoming a superstar. 'I just wanted to acknowledge all of the many layers of myself, which I think is definitely something that comes with age,' she told *The Face*. 'Obviously, after a really big life moment, like my divorce, it's good to experiment a little bit more with sort of eclectic inspirations. I wanted to, more than anything, just comfort myself. It wasn't really about what I wanted to say for people. It was more like: What do I need to hear for myself, lyrically?'

Starting on 1 October 2021, billboards and light displays began to hint that a new Adele album was imminent. Light projections carrying the number 30 started appearing at notable spots around the world, such as Buckingham Palace, the Eiffel Tower, the Empire State Building, the Colosseum and the Louvre. Three days later, Adele changed all her social media profile images to a navy blue photo and also updated her website to match with a new logo and branding. On 13 October, the news became official when Adele announced the album via social media, confirming both the title *30* and the release date of 19 November 2021. The following day, *30* was made available for pre-order in CD, digital, LP (two black vinyl discs) and cassette formats on her personal website.

Meanwhile, behind the scenes, Adele was feeling the pressure of the surge in attention that she would face as the new album was released. 'Umm, definitely a bit overwhelmed,' she told *The Face*, when asked how she felt. 'Everything's beginning to launch and stuff like that, but [I'm] also trying to remember that I feel like this every time a record comes out, you know? So it's like, it goes from zero to a hundred in a matter of weeks, because I don't do anything for so long.'

It would prove to be a monumental piece of work, as was noted stylishly by one reviewer. 'Grappling with guilt, shame and insecurity over her recent divorce yet infused with a life-affirming sense of liberation, self-forgiveness and burgeoning new romance,' Adele had made 'what might just be the most potent everywoman album since Carole King's 1971 classic *Tapestry*,' wrote Neil McCormick in the *Daily Telegraph*.

The potency began right from the first line of *30*. 'I'll be taking flowers to the cemetery of my heart,' is quite a powerful opening line for a track. As an opening line for an album, it is even more compelling. With this song, 'Strangers by Nature', Adele is channelling her inner Judy Garland and doing so with some style, backed by bittersweet Disney-esque strings. The core message of the song is that we are strangers to another. This is a pre-rock'n'roll ballad on which Adele positively croons the words. It is one of two tracks on the album in which Adele's delivery is scented with a slight perfume of Amy Winehouse. Curiously, the way she says, at the end of the track, 'All right then, I'm ready,' suggests she sees this as a prologue to the album as much as a part of it.

But what was she ready for? We begin to discover in 'Easy on Me'. The lead single from the album, it is reminiscent of Elton John and goes strong on the confessional theme of the album. She pleads that she was still just a child and urges her former lover to go easy on her. She insists she tried hard and points out that they were both set in their ways. Taking the theme even further, she says that she changed who she was for 'both of you' but has now given up. Nevertheless, she concedes, her 'good intentions' and 'highest hopes' don't show. 'Easy on Me' was produced by Greg Kurstin, who, as we have seen, already had an impressive discography.

Next on the album is 'My Little Love', the most atmospheric track on 30 and, arguably, out of all of Adele's material. It is also her most controversial song to date. A classic soul track, its melodies are truly overpowering, but the overall feeling is one of intense intimacy. It is bleak and long, with elements of trip hop and seventies groove, with a dash of Marvin Gaye. It has a soporific, almost lullaby feel, a near seven-minute track of maternal pangs.

It is disquieting, unsettling, even. But that is the intended effect – Adele has not included those voice notes to do anything but push some boundaries. But perhaps the real reason we are unsettled is not that she has tapped into such deep emotion but that she is able to do it so well and with such depth. In this era of over-sharing on social media, lots of people are 'opening their book' more widely than usual, but few can do it with the artistry of Adele. It as if she has cast her gaze upon a billion tweets and posts and decided to show us how it is done. Angelo is not the only one whose eyes widen like an ocean. There are early signs that he is something of a poet. Asked during 'My Little Love' to tell his mother he loves her, he replies: 'I love you a million per cent.' As we have seen, he also once told his mother he 'couldn't see' her. These quotes suggest great depths.

'Cry Your Heart Out' comes next. Its blend of multiple genres, including Motown, rhythm and blues, and reggae, along with the deliberate distortion of Adele's vocals, give this lyrically sad song a rather carefree lift. It has been described by one reviewer as 'the musical equivalent of putting on a brave face when it feels literally impossible to do so'. Who cannot relate to such a moment? The slick piano key progressions really add to the satisfaction, but this remains one of the less remarked upon of Adele's tracks on *30*. Nevertheless, the healing power of a good cry cannot be denied, and so Adele's advice in this song is good and sound.

The bass and whistles that are added to the production of 'Oh My God' take this track to a whole new level and rocket it to the sort of ultra-commercial territory that marked it out for obvious release as a single. It deals with her inner conflict over whether to have fun or not. Her defiance and refusal to explain herself, or to not do what feels right, steadily emerge and, as she teeters on the edge of heaven and hell, the effect is brilliant for her listeners.

The video for 'Oh My God' was directed by Sam Brown, who previously worked with her on the video for 'Rolling in the Deep'. It managed to absolutely wow fans and set off a tidal wave of discussion and speculation over what the richly symbolic promotional video was trying to tell us. The *Daily Mail* said it 'commands attention' thanks to Adele's pellegrina cape. It was certainly a stylish affair that saw her dressed in a number of vintage-inspired outfits by designers including Vivienne Westwood, Harris Reed and Louis Vuitton. Set in a contemporary Garden of Eden, there are multiple dancers and several apples, including in a scene in which Adele is sitting on a chair and taking a bite of an apple.

Adele has described 'Oh My God' as her 'hot mess' song which explores her navigating leaving her marriage and life post-divorce. The fact that in the video she sat on and then burned a chair led to much online speculation. Devoted fans noted that she had sung from a chair in the videos for 'Hometown Glory', 'Rolling in the Deep' and 'Easy on Me'. Therefore, the fact the chair in 'Oh My God' was set alight meant to some that she was moving on, burning the very prop that dominated past videos.

As she sang 'I won't leave myself behind' on the video a boy is playing with apples in the background. This was widely viewed as a reference to maintaining a strong relationship with herself and Angelo. When a dancer sat on the floor picking daisy petals, this seemed to be a nod to the childhood daisy-picking game 'He loves me, he loves me not'. Did the flower represent the fragility of her marriage? With two dancers intertwined on a mattress, the video is notably more sexual than anything she had put out before.

'Can I Get It' is another highly commercial track – here, too, there are whistles, but they are bolder and more aligned to the beat. A pop classic co-written with pop pros Max Martin and Shellback, it introduces more rhythm and blues sounds and deals again with internal conflict. 'It sounds like a newly free divorcee trying a bit too hard to convince herself she's having fun,' said the *Evening Standard*. It has been compared heavily to Ed Sheeran's material. It has also been described – or dismissed? – as a pop filler by some critics, but when those syncopated whistles are blasting out, few will be able to resist its lure.

The next song on *30*, 'I Drink Wine', has perhaps the best title of any Adele track to date, and the song itself does not disappoint either. However, anyone expecting it to be a happy celebration of partying will be surprised when they find heavy, weary lyrics. She questions how life gradually erodes our essence, turning us into a version of someone we do not even like. She loves the world but feels that the world only wants to bring her down, corrupting her mind with negative ideas. Whereas as a child she soaked up all of life and existence, now she only soaks up wine, she laments.

Along the way, she also questions if anyone is satisfied by life. She berates herself for becoming obsessed with things she has no control over and for craving the approval of strangers. She fears that even as she grows, she will be none the wiser about life's mysteries but, as the title tells us, she can drink wine. Musically, this is all set to a wonderful power ballad that reminds us of Elton John's earlier material. He looms increasingly large in her sound. It will be great fun for fans to sing along to this at concerts.

During the song she sings of making memories in a storm. She explained to *The Face* that this was a reference to a man who she 'loved' and had 'been fond of' who had suggested they have a relationship after she broke up with Simon Konecki. 'I couldn't give myself properly,' she said. 'I couldn't be consistent, and neither could he. It wasn't right, leaving a marriage and then dating a year after. Even if you feel ready, it's a gaping, open wound whether you leave or you're left. So it was more that this person was asking for me to throw myself into it. And I couldn't because I was still recovering from the breakdown of my marriage.' She said she associates this man with 'the storm' of that time. 'I was just, you know, really honest with him about it, thank God,' she continued. 'Otherwise I could've found myself in a situation being in a relationship I didn't want to be in after coming out of one.'

On *30*'s next song, 'All Night Parking (With Erroll Garner)', it is as if Ella Fitzgerald has made a twenty-first-century jazz track. It evokes visions of Adele singing in a classic jazz bar, only partially viewable amid the smoke from cigarettes and cigars. The seductive production makes this a great rendering of a rare territory for Adele – it is not about heartache for a past lover but about the quiet excitement of a new love. Using a backing track from the Pittsburgh jazz pianist Erroll Garner, who died in 1977, the sleepy romance of this track is beautiful. Amy Winehouse would have loved to sing such a track, and we would have loved her to sing it to us. That said, Adele singing it is perfection. Marked as an 'Interlude', this soporific two-minute track is a gem. Anyone who has yearned to spend every moment of their time with a new love will ease into this song as if they are sliding into a beautiful bath. Rarely has new love sounded so gently thrilling.

In 'Woman Like Me' Adele is addressing a lazy new lover who hasn't met her expectations. It is a sassy manifesto against complacency that has been described by her as a 'diss track'. She told *Rolling Stone* the song was about a relationship she had after her divorce and said, 'even though I'm directing all the things I'm saying at someone else, they're also things I've learned on this journey. The storyline of what I'm saying, I wouldn't have been able to write before because it was something that I was experiencing myself.' However, some felt it was simultaneously a challenge to Adele's audience to re-evaluate how they see her.

Speaking of the song's producer, she told *The Face*, 'We just really got on, and the chords and cadences that he has in his bank – I've never heard anything like it. He's the coolest guy. There's something about Scandinavians that's different. I don't know where they get their f***ing ideas from but they are incredible.' In fact, the GRAMMY- and Oscar-winning Swedish music producer Ludwig Göransson, who worked with Adele on this track, is rumoured to have made an impact on her life beyond music.

A source told a tabloid newspaper that Adele began working with him at around the time her marriage to Simon Konecki was ending. 'She has said often in the past that when she is going through something difficult the studio is her safe place, and this was no exception,' the unnamed source said. 'She and Ludwig developed a close friendship and they shared some very intense, late-night conversations about their lives and relationships.' There is no suggestion that their bond was in any way romantic – he was then engaged to his now wife, the violinist Serena McKinney.

'Hold On', the next song on 30, is one of the standout tracks both of the album and of Adele's career. This gospel-tinged song sees Adele backed by a beautiful choir. In a time when mental health problems are rocketing among the young, the lyrics of the track could prove a godsend for some listeners who are entertaining ideas of suicide. If so, then lyrically and thematically, this track could be Adele's greatest contribution to the world.

Then, in the track 'To Be Loved', she sounds like Whitney Houston. This beautiful piano ballad is considered by some to be Adele's best vocal performance of her career. The song's lyrics find Adele reflecting how young she was during her failed marriage, addressing a future version of her son, explaining her divorce and finding the path to happiness again. Some felt that this song, more than the others, defines 30.

Wrote one critic, Adele reaches a 'testimonial finale so big that she sounds as if she might blow out her vocal cord'.

He added that the track reached a climax that was 'shocking to hear', with the 'raw emotion accomplishing something beyond musical finesse'. He said that 'compared with the youthful heartaches that inspired earlier albums, this is the motherload', but added that there was also 'plenty of spirited positivity amid the self-pity and self-flagellation', lines that were 'delivered with Adele's customary gusto and lit up by her sheer joy when singing'. The final crescendo of 'I tried' is so powerful and emotional that some have considered it shocking. The AllMusic website said it was a 'shiver-inducing showcase of vocal acrobatics that stands tall alongside the best performances by Whitney, Mariah, and Celine'.

That would have made for a dramatic, and somewhat dark, closer for 30, but there is one more track to come. Here, gorgeous strings and a pensive organ bring in a cinematic, Motown girl-group flavour. Amy Winehouse sang that 'Love Is a Losing Game'. Adele's song title 'Love Is a Game' is one word short of that, but this track is very much a song you could imagine Winehouse singing so well. It may not be an album closer on a par with 'Someone Like You', but for many ears it outclasses 'Sweetest Devotion' from 25, and possibly 'Hometown Glory' from 19.

Neil McCormick of the the *Daily Telegraph*, an old fan of Adele, was wowed by 30. His only issue with the collection was whether Adele was 'guilty of oversharing'. He felt the 'weepy voice notes may be a bit too much' and wondered whether we 'really needed to hear home recordings of Adele laying all her woes on her own child ... or blubbering into her phone during bouts of insecurity'. However, he still felt this was her 'strongest album yet' – a work of 'catharsis, therapy and succour'.

The Times cheered that 'Adele's voice remains remarkable: pure and unaffected, with that extremely rare ability of hers to convey big drama, small intimacy and throwaway humour all at once'. The newspaper's critic added that 'there is nothing here that offends or jars, no blatant attempts to jump on trends, no streaming numbers-aware collaborations with big rappers or pop stars'.

Journalist Annabel Nugent felt that the Adele of *30* is 'more literal' than previous incarnations, describing her this time round as 'Adele unmediated. Adele unfiltered.' Writing for the *Independent*, she added that *30* has 'happier love songs' because, 'unlike her previous records, which can be wearisome in excess … *30* is more diverse in its psychological palette'. She also thought that the new album was more inward-looking than its predecessors. 'Where other records have asked for audience participation – for us to fill in the blanks of broad narratives with our own pain – *30* is a conversation between Adele and Adele,' she concluded.

'As she sings, the biggest musician in the world frequently sounds extraordinarily vulnerable,' wrote David Smyth in the *Evening Standard*. 'It no longer sounds like she's making music to achieve towering sales figures. At times, her fans will wonder why someone who has guarded her privacy so fiercely has shared some of these nakedly despairing songs at all.'

Simon Boyle of the *Sun* said that 'despite much of *30* being devoted to lost love and personal disappointments, it is rarely a challenging listen' because 'low moments [are] interspersed with enough up-tempo beats to prompt involuntary head nodding and toe-tapping reminiscent of some of her earlier fan favourites'. He declared that 'every line paints a picture, and I feel like I've watched a movie', adding that 'this is a blockbuster – from a true Hollywood superstar'.

The *Daily Mail* said that *30* was a 'barnstorming return'. Adrian Thrills added that 'at the heart of it all, of course, is that dazzling, blue-eyed soul voice – emotional without being cloying – and her phrasing is as impeccable as ever here'. However, the *Guardian* was not so sure. Lead reviewer Alexis Petridis said that some fans 'might find themselves wishing she'd occasionally give it a rest about how hard she tried and how much she's cried', particularly during 'To Be Loved', which 'feels as if it lasts for about six weeks'.

In a separate, later article for the same newspaper, music writer Laura Snapes noted that 'critics have often justified Adele's era-defining success by her relatability, but the daring woman on *30* is a provocation; the pop equivalent of Glennon Doyle, the self-help guru whose work made Adele feel "as if I just flew into my body for the very first time".' For *NME*, *30* was an album of 'mixed results'. El Hunt wrote that the 'hit-rate' in her songs 'isn't a hundred per cent'. The music weekly gave the album just three out of five stars – a rare exception to the avalanche of four-star and five-star ratings that *30* received.

Across the pond, *Rolling Stone* was firmly in the five-star camp. 'Adele has never sounded more ferocious than she does on *30* – more alive to her own feelings, more virtuosic at shaping them into songs in the key of her own damn life,' wrote Rob Sheffield. 'It's her toughest, most powerful album yet.' *Variety* felt that 'there's a bracing maturity in these twelve tracks that's more emotionally complex and intriguing than the rather more easy-to-follow woe of the preceding three collections'.

The Atlantic magazine said that 'some of her choices ... aren't the ones all of her listeners might have craved' but '*30* generally blazes because Adele, with all the power and talent anyone could ask for, is doing exactly what she wants'. Writing for *The Sunday Times*, Dan Cairns said that it seemed as if *30* had 'the ingredients for a classic break-up album. . . On paper, yes. In reality, alas, not quite.' He wrote that the album's first half 'mixes the familiar with the unexpected' with a 'welcome breeziness that ensnares you afresh'. In the first half, he added, we find 'the Adele we first fell for' but 'part two of *30* is essentially Meghan-meets-Oprah in song'. He complained about the 'Californiacation of Adele's phonetics' and how she 'succumbs to mindful, Malibu-hoo therapy speak and Goopy, happy-clappy platitudes'. Turning the knife somewhat, he said that, while he listened to 'To Be Loved', 'Two phrases in my notes read "Please stop singing" and "Move on, jeez".' He concluded that 'LA has claimed Adele as its own. Time, surely, for Tottenham to stage a fightback.'

Three weeks before its release, *30* was already making history. The album broke the Apple Music record for the most pre-added album ever on the streaming platform, surpassing Billie Eilish's *Happier Than Ever*. It also broke the record for the largest number of pre-adds in a single day, as well as the record for achieving it in the shortest timeframe.

Speaking about the album, Adele was in proud and ebullient mood. It was clear she was pleased with the final product. 'There's not an occasion or a scenario or a feeling where there is not the perfect song for it somewhere,' she said. Discussing the songs, she told Apple Music 1 radio station: 'I really think that some of the songs on this album could really help people, really change people's lives. And I think a song like "Hold On" could actually save a few lives. I really, really do.'

Turning to 'My Little Love', she said it was inspired by a remarkable conversation between her and Angelo. Remembering the time the exchange happened, she said, 'I was present in real life, but I just wasn't really there. I was just so consumed ... by so many things, to be honest with you, so many different feelings.'

This was where her son came in, she explained. 'And he plucked up the courage to very articulately say to me, "You're basically a ghost. You might as well not be here." When he said, "I can't see you." And I'm like, what kind of poet is that?' A nine-year-old poet. Adele continued: 'For him to be little and say, "I can't see you," to my face broke my heart. And I just … that was definitely one of the things I was most scared of when I left our … I didn't leave our family, but left that structure, was just, what if he hates me forever?' As she wrote the song, she said she remembered 'thinking of any child that's been through divorce or any person that has been through a divorce themselves or anyone that wants to leave a relationship and never will'.

The personal focus Adele allowed herself with *30* might be intensified on future material. *Vogue* thought that we can expect Adele's music to become more inward-gazing in the future. The magazine said she was 'done with lambasting her exes in her lyrics', quoting the singer as saying, 'I have to really address myself now.'

Expanding on the theme, Adele had told the magazine: 'I was drunk as a fart on *21*; I really don't remember much, I just remember being really sad,' she said. 'On *25*, I was obviously sober as anything, because I was a new mum. That one, I was sort of more in tune with what I thought people might want or not want. With this one, I made the very conscious decision to be like, for the first time in my life, actually, "What do I want?" I feel like this album is self-destruction, then self-reflection and then sort of self-redemption,' she said. 'But I feel ready. I really want people to hear my side of the story this time.'

They heard it in large numbers. Over in America, it debuted at Number One on the *Billboard* chart. However, as *The New York Times*' headline pointed out, it failed to shift a million units in its first week of release in the US, though its sales figure of 839,000 was more than respectable, comprising 692,000 sold as complete packages – CDs or vinyl LPs, etc. This meant it beat the first-week sales of both Drake's *Certified Lover Boy* and Taylor Swift's *Red (Taylor's Version)* by more than 200,000. In addition, its songs racked up 185 million streams. However, it remained significantly lower in sales than Adele's last album, 25, which caused such a stir throughout the industry by selling nearly 3.4 million copies in its first week alone.

It had been quite the event but, of all the thousands of words written about *30*, one sentiment would continue to echo longer than the others: the idea that LA had 'taken' Adele and that Tottenham needed to reclaim her. To some, these words may seem like typical British parochialism – a resentment that one of our number had seemingly become 'too big for their boots' over in the US. However, in 2021 a definite backlash grew against Adele and in 2022 it would erupt into a drama that hogged the headlines for days, leaving some observers wondering what had become of the shy girl from London.

CHAPTER NINE

NEW BEGINNINGS

Anyone who hits the heights of success, fame and fortune will reach a point when some in the media turn against them. Reporters and commentators will happily build you up and then knock you down. It's what they do. To an extent, Adele had managed to be protected from this trend for longer than most because her sparse media appearances meant that she was in the sights of journalists less than most stars. However, she began to feel some negativity after her appearance with Oprah Winfrey in November 2021. This prime-time special show in the US was Adele's first TV interview about her new album.

It also saw her perform a selection of new songs and classic hits at the scenic Griffith Observatory in Los Angeles, in the shadow of the Hollywood sign. It was filmed at twilight, adding to the atmosphere. During the broadcast, Adele even helped a local man propose to his girlfriend. After the bride-to-be said yes, Adele serenaded the couple with 'Make You Feel My Love'. 'Thank God she said "Yes", because I didn't know who I was going to sing this song to next,' Adele quipped.

Stars like Lizzo, James Corden and Melissa McCarthy were in the small audience for the twilight concert, which was the first time Adele's young son, Angelo, had seen her perform live. The show was entertaining and was lapped up by Adele's fans. It was exciting for them to see their heroine again, hear her new material and get the chance to catch up with the latest twists and turns of her private life.

However, some critics in the UK found fault with the show and its star guest. It seemed that there had been a simmering resentment in the UK over Adele's new, more LA lifestyle. With the release of 30 and the promotional drive that went with it, that resentment began to boil over. Commentators began to question whether Adele had become too big for her boots. Sarah Ditum in the *Daily Telegraph* complained that Adele's words 'sounded suspiciously like La-La Land therapy talk'. Ditum wrote that, when asked about how she coped with the heartbreak of deciding to end her marriage, Adele spoke of 'the process of arriving to yourself every single day, turning up to yourself every single day', and described how she was 'trying to move forward with intention'.

'Adele's vocabulary has all the hallmarks of someone who's spent much of the six years since her last record "processing",' said Ditum. The writer observed that 'Adele's persona is of someone who's just like us' but added that 'inevitably, massive success means she's becoming one of them'. A similar observation had been made when Adele made a video with *Vogue*. As a game, she was blindfolded in a café, and asked to identify classic British delicacies. She correctly named the pork pie and cockles, but when she ate chips she identified them as 'fries'. For some, this was further evidence that Adele had ... changed. Ditum sniffed that Adele had lost herself 'in the Hollywood bubble', which means 'she can't carry on being the gobby London girl the world fell in love with' because 'Adele belongs to Los Angeles now'. This disdain for a British celebrity who makes it big in America is not new; the parochialism of some on these shores is offended by anyone who makes it big across the pond. Therefore, Ditum's complaints were probably inevitable.

However, the *Daily Telegraph*'s reaction was a thing of restraint compared to Janet Street-Porter's verdict. 'I love Adele's voice,' began the veteran columnist in the *Daily Mail*. 'Her live performances are electrifying. But please, please, please spare me any more of her talking.' Street-Porter objected to 'the fake misery, the gushing tears on tap every hour and the vacuousness of her bright shiny life in sunny California ... blah blah blah'. She said Adele was responsible for a 'tidal wave of waffle and wallow' during the Oprah interview.

Like Ditum, the *Daily Mail* columnist looked favourably upon the past Adele but only to set her up against the present-day Adele. 'In her teens and twenties, Adele was adorable –

brash, loud, madly enthusiastic,' she wrote. She didn't like the singer's 'brash' new look and felt that 'the more she gushes, the less I love her'. Attempting to hitch her attack on Adele onto the anti-Meghan bandwagon, Street-Porter said, 'Can you any longer tell the difference between Meghan Markle and Adele Adkins? Both had difficult relationships with their fathers and worship their mothers. Both felt that Oprah was the best person to share their "truths" with.' In fairness, Adele's interview with Oprah did take place in the same California rose garden as Markle and Harry's had, but this still felt like a contrived comparison.

Indeed, the *Daily Mail* was not content with one opinionated columnist taking aim at Adele. The *Mail*'s notorious writer Jan Moir also set her sights on Adele – and this time, the connection with Oprah's previous headline-hitting interview was made clear from the first sentence. 'And lo, once more we come to the Garden of Oprah, just as the disciples Harry and Meghan cameth before us and verily spoke their truth before the tree of knowledge and the fount of Winfrey,' wrote Moir, who hit the headlines herself in 2009, when her article about the death of Boyzone singer Stephen Gately was described in the *Guardian* as a 'gratuitous piece of gay-bashing'.

Noting the host and guest's similar outfits, Moir said 'Oprah and Adele looked as if they had just married each other on a Malibu beach, or were perhaps job-sharing a senior receptionist position in a Las Vegas wellness spa.' (Other media outlets were more impressed with the two women's matching neutral outfits, even offering tips for where viewers could buy similar garments of their own.) Moir went on to note that Adele 'was on her best behaviour and didn't swear once, which was a miracle', but 'to be honest with ya, as Adele would say,' Moir continued, 'there was very little that seemed truly spontaneous in their manicured exchanges'.

Where Ditum and Street-Porter complained that Adele was not down-to-earth enough, Moir felt that 'if there is one criticism to be made of Adele, it is that she can overdo the downhome dudeness ... even in all her grand silk gown glory in Griffith Park, she was drinking a mug of tea and coming over all lawks-a-daisy Eliza Doolittle between songs'. Here, at least, was proof that you cannot please them all.

Piers Morgan also weighed in on the backlash, perhaps inevitably. Commenting on *30*, he sniffed that Adele had 'gone back on her word not to do another break-up album, and her vow not to be a "bitter witch"', and also criticized the 'curious movable feast of her privacy'. He compared the album's songs with the statement that was put out by Adele's team to announce her separation from Konecki. 'As always they ask for privacy,' the team's statement ended. 'There will be no further comment.' Morgan raged that it 'turns out there was going to be a lot of "further comment" about the marriage, in fact, a whole album full of it', adding: 'I can just imagine the wails of outrage that would have burst from that fabulous set of pipes if anyone in the media had trashed her husband as a complacent, lazy and uncaring man.'

He also complained about the voice note conversations with Angelo included in 'My Little Love'. 'This is the same Adele who went to court to protect her son's privacy when he was just one, winning him a substantial five-figure sum in damages over paparazzi photographs,' he wrote. Accusing her of hypocrisy, he said of her soul-bearing album, 'she's done it for attention, money, and sales'.

Morgan, like many media commentators, often accuses stars of hypocrisy when they reveal details of their private lives on their own terms, after blocking the attempts of tabloids to expose details on their terms. It is easy to be seduced by his argument, but is it really so contradictory for a singer to create art that expresses her heartache while preferring for salacious tabloids to not invade her privacy and twist what they find?

Elsewhere, the verdicts on her Oprah slot were more positive. The *Evening Standard* said Adele 'came up with the goods' in the TV special; NBC News said she 'got candid'. *The Times* enjoyed the 'brutal honesty and heartbreak songs' and pointed out that, unlike Meghan's interview, Adele was not seeking to rehabilitate her image by sitting down with Oprah. Whatever the critics thought of the show, it was a hit with the viewers. An average of 9.9 million viewers tuned in to watch, according to *The Hollywood Reporter*. The special scored higher than 2021's Academy Awards, which took in just 9.85 million viewers. It was also a good money-spinner for the network. The *Mirror* claimed that the CBS show could generate more than $100 million (over £74 million), with James Corden's production company expected to take a cut. The two-hour special did not come cheap. An insider claimed that CBS had paid 'at least $5 million, but perhaps as much as $7 million' to host the interview.

There was a lesser tremor of backlash after her special show on the UK's ITV later the same month. It was attended by a veritable Who's Who of UK celebrities, including Dame Emma Thompson, Stormzy and Idris Elba. Also present were Olly Alexander, Gareth Southgate, Dawn French, Kate Garraway, Jonathan Ross, Graham Norton and Alan Carr. As one critic put it, the crowd at the London Palladium 'seemed to contain every celebrity within a hundred square miles'.

After Adele launched the show with an emotional performance of 'Hometown Glory' – with the second verse's expletive removed – she remarked a few times about how 'emotional' and 'nervous' she was. At one point on the night, she restarted her performance of 'Easy on Me' after becoming emotional on the first attempt. Or as Adele put it: 'one more time, I'm s****ing myself'.

Piers Morgan, not satisfied with his recent tirade against Adele's supposed 'hypocrisy' waded in again, but this time he faced quite a backlash. The opinionated journalist came under fire after his online comments about the show when he spoke out on Twitter as the special played out. He tweeted: 'If I was at this #AnAudienceWithAdele, I'd ask her two questions: 1) Does the unctuous sycophancy from your celebrity fans make you want to vomit? 2) How come you're singing more perfectly "live" than on your records?' He faced a host of criticism for his remarks, with many people tweeting comments such as 'Tell me you're upset you weren't invited to the Adele special without telling me you're upset you weren't invited to the Adele special.' Another Twitter user asked, 'Why can't you just celebrate and enjoy such a wonderful British success story? What is wrong with you?' A third tweet commented, 'Are you ever not dragging a woman down? Sitting behind your keyboard and berating any woman in the spotlight.'

What happened next is, perhaps, testimony to Adele's influence. Normally, when Morgan is taken to task for his criticism of a famous female, he doubles down and insists he is right, shrugging off any disapproval of his stance. In this case, however, when he returned to Twitter it was with a more contrite message. 'Minor irritations aside, there's no doubt that @Adele is the best singer in the world right now & right up there with Barbra & Whitney as possessor of the best set of pipes in pop history,' he wrote.

This was neither an apology nor a direct acknowledgement of wrongdoing, but the world has learned not to hold its breath waiting for either of those from Morgan. However, it was an uncharacteristically tame comment from the bombastic Morgan. The man who had taken to task countless celebs on Twitter had seemingly realized he had picked a fight with the wrong person this time.

Back at the London Palladium, everyone was having a lovely night. In between her triumphant performances of songs old and new, Adele held question-and-answer slots with her famous audience. When asked who she'd like to collaborate with, Adele did not reply with the name of a musician but instead singled out the actor Daniel Kaluuya, who was then best known for his roles in *Queen & Slim* and *Black Panther*. He was present at the London Palladium performance and looked shocked and humbled as Adele told him, 'I just want to watch you work, I think I'd learn a lot.'

When Adele was asked by the actress Hannah Waddingham who her idol is, many expected the answer to be Beyoncé. She did indeed acknowledge that the diva is 'one of her favourites' but explained that when it comes to idols, the two standout names are Bette Midler and Barbra Streisand.

The actor Idris Elba asked her, 'You've inspired singers, you've created incredible albums – what's one tiny moment that you're most proud of?' She replied that it was overcoming anxiety and performing at the Glastonbury Festival. The comedian Alan Carr asked Adele, 'If one of your exes wrote a song about you, what would it be called and what would it sound like?' Adele quipped: 'It'd probably be called "No One Like You", I imagine.' The audience fell about laughing.

Asked by the rapper Stormzy whether she had ever felt awkward when she'd met an idol, she said she had when she met Stevie Nicks. 'I'm just a huge Fleetwood Mac fan – I love their melodies. I was pretty chilled out about going to see her in concert, but the moment I met her, I started crying and she had to go into icon mode and be like, "Oh, it's alright."'

There was an awkward moment when former Spice Girl, Mel B, asked a question about the best gift Adele had ever received but added a quip that she could answer the question for Adele, and said it was a vibrator. According to eyewitnesses, this led to an uncomfortable moment, since nobody found it amusing. 'No one really laughed but Adele made a wisecrack about it and moved on,' they said.

The *Mirror* said that another guest enjoying an uncomfortable evening was Phillip Schofield, who was 'left gutted' after being seated behind Boy George and his 'massive hat'. Boy George was, indeed, wearing a huge, round blue hat, and after Schofield was spotted trying to gaze round the headgear, the TV presenter was later seen in a better spot.

Dame Emma Thompson posed a heart-warming question of Adele, asking, 'When you were younger, was there anyone who inspired you, protected you from all the trials and tribulations of the world?' Adele answered that it was her English teacher, Ms McDonald. 'She taught English, but she also taught street dancing,' said Adele. 'She was so bloody cool, engaging, and she really made us care and made us feel like she really cared. She was so likable and relatable, and actually made me like her.' Next, Ms McDonald was ushered up on stage, to the apparent surprise of Adele. Some cynics suggested that the moment had been engineered, but whether it had been or not, it made for emotional television.

'What becomes very clear very quickly is that this is the ideal vehicle for Adele,' wrote Rachel Aroesti of the *Guardian*, because she is 'known as a chronically no-nonsense, compulsively self-deprecating Londoner with a great sense of humour'. The critic said Adele was 'ridiculously quick-witted' and radiated 'relatability', adding that she 'surpassed whatever expectations anyone might have had of her hosting skills: it's hard to imagine anybody doing this better'. Katie Rosseinsky of the *Evening Standard* said Adele 'has more than enough charisma and candour to ease things along' and delivered anecdotes 'like she's regaling a bunch of friends in the pub'. Rosseinsky concluded that 'this was a triumphant return from an artist at the very top of her game, who still manages to feel like your mate from school – it's wonderful to have her back'.

Although the critics mostly welcomed the show, even here there was a hint of the simmering backlash against Adele. The *Daily Telegraph* contrasted the Adele we saw here with the Adele of the Oprah show. 'The yoga mat had … been left behind as she came to London,' wrote the paper's Ed Power. 'This was the Adele the world had fallen in love with: melodramatic but endearingly earthbound. She sang like a turbocharged diva and chatted between songs in the style of a neighbour who'd poked their head over the hedge with some juicy gossip to share.' Like many a backlash, the feeling was that the media would accept the version of Adele that they approved of – the fat, shy singer of the *19* and *21* eras, but not the even more successful and up-to-date version.

They say that all publicity is good publicity, but that received wisdom would be stretched to its limits by the steadily growing controversy that surrounded Adele as 2021 came to an end and 2022 began. The promotion for *30* was to be a truly rocky ride. The album became the centre of an internationally awkward story when an Australian journalist's interview with Adele was canned because he did not listen to *30* before flying across the globe to interview her about it. Matt Doran, of Channel 7 News, jetted to London ahead of the album's release, and after he had finished the interview, Adele discovered that he had not listened to a preview, claiming he had 'missed' the email which contained a link to it. Her record label, Sony, duly blocked the interview from airing. It was reported that the deal for the interview and rights to other related content cost the channel a million Australian dollars – around £530,000.

This story became huge and, speaking later on Channel 7, Doran held his hands up. 'Now I want to address something that's made headlines this week and something that I would like to apologize for,' began his mea culpa. He described it as a 'story that has sparked a torrent of abuse and mockery from around the world', adding that 'the bulk of this savaging I deserve and I totally own'. He explained that he made the 'terrible mistake' of 'assuming we weren't to be given a preview copy of this album, because our interview was airing before it was released and Adele's album was the industry's most prized secret'.

He said that, contrary to rumours, Adele had not walked out of the interview, which he described as an 'unspeakable privilege'. However, he added, 'by missing the album link –

however I might try to justify it – I've insulted Adele'. He added that 'I'd never have knowingly disrespected you by deliberately not listening to your work. I am so sorry.'

He faced a lot of criticism, but also some support, including from comedian and columnist David Mitchell. 'You'd have to be chronically deficient in empathy not to feel sorry for Australian TV reporter Matt Doran,' he wrote in the *Observer*, 'I suspect he's currently discovering quite how many people on the internet suffer from that condition.' *The Sunday Times*' Camilla Long cast a weary eye over the controversy and asked, 'Have we all gone mad?' She continued that 'crawling to a primadonna who's thrown a pathetic tantrum is something I expect from North Korea … Adele should be embarrassed for participating in such an orgy of greed-driven fakery.'

All of this was indeed good business for Adele. In December 2021, it was reported that she had earned £28 million in one year from the two companies that bank the takings from her recording career. The *Daily Mail* reported that Melted Stone Publishing Ltd, which was formed in April 2011, showed cash in the bank and in hand at £8,941,779 after costs of £4,518,566. Meanwhile, Melted Stone Ltd, which was formed in April 2008, showed cash in the bank and in hand at £19,996,938.

Adele was on the brink of making even tidier sums thanks to a planned Las Vegas concert residency, 'Weekends with Adele'. However, what might have been a dream experience for Adele and her fans abruptly turned into a nightmare for both. Adele was about to experience her most controversial moment to date, one that was to leave some observers wondering whatever had happened to the sweet down-to-earth girl from Tottenham.

It was supposed to be a unifying experience. Coming after two years in which the live music sector was effectively on hold due to the Covid pandemic, Adele's shows in Las Vegas would offer a great chance for her and her fans to be together. There would be an intimacy to the performances, in common with all residencies. Everyone would be a winner.

According to reports, she would make up to $2 million per show at the territory which has proven so lucrative for the likes of Britney Spears, Lady Gaga and Katy Perry. As Frank Sinatra once put it: 'Las Vegas is the only place I know where money really talks. It says, "Goodbye."' However, as *The Times* once pointed out, if you're a music star, 'it says a sunny, "Hello! Can I introduce you to a lorry load of my friends?"' For evidence of this look no further than Celine Dion, whose Vegas residencies from 2003 to 2007 and from 2011 to 2019 generated more than half a billion pounds in ticket sales.

For Adele, the draw of Vegas was as much about convenience as commerce. She hated the travelling involved in long tours, particularly the air travel. She also wanted to be near her son, who would be only an hour's flight away in Los Angeles. That said, there are undoubtedly also downsides to Vegas residencies. The dry, desert air of Nevada can make life difficult for vocalists. Adele was strongly advised to install humidifiers in her room. Also, some artists felt that a Vegas residency was a white flag. For example, Paul McCartney told *GQ* that playing Vegas was 'something I've been trying to avoid my whole life. Definitely nothing attracts me about the idea. It's the elephants' graveyard.' Cher once said of her audiences in Vegas: 'They're not allowed to stand up and they're very, very old. Sometimes they had walkers and oxygen masks. It took me a long time to realize that it may be the last concert they ever see.'

However, for Adele, there was much to recommend the audiences who come to Vegas. These crowds generally enjoy a slower pace to shows and plenty of humorous interaction between songs. *Billboard* reported that she would play twice a weekend from 21 January to 16 April 2022 at the Colosseum at Caesars Palace. Many of the tickets, which sold out in about six hours, did not come cheap. The music industry journal reported that ticket prices ranged from $5,000 each for the front three rows in the orchestra from Ticketmaster's platinum program; $860 each for the Colosseum's front section; and $600 for the front portion of the upper balcony at the venue. However, some tickets were priced as cheap as $85, according to the report.

Fans on social media were livid when the expensive tickets sold out quickly, with some then reappearing on resale websites. 'Adele out her rabbit ass mind with these concert ticket prices,' wrote one. Then there was a controversy when it was revealed that Covid vaccination and a negative test would be required for anyone to gain entry to the venue. A notice on the Ticketmaster website read: 'Both proof of vaccination AND proof of a negative test within 48 hours of the event is required to enter the event.' She had previously expressed her concerns about coronavirus, saying, 'it's too unpredictable'. She added: 'I don't want anyone coming to my show scared. And I don't want to get Covid, either.'

But according to the *Sun*, the shows would make her one of the highest-paid female stars in the history of Las Vegas residencies. She would reportedly pocket a cut from all merchandise sold at the 4,200-seater venue. She was also said to be treated to a host of perks with Caesars laying on a £30,000-a-night private suite accessible at any time during the residency, a butler, executive assistant, chauffeur and security.

There were headlines attacking Adele for the steep Vegas ticket prices. These criticisms echoed similar upset about prices when Adele announced a number of shows in London's Hyde Park for the summer of 2022. The tickets were expensive in the first place – such as the £580 price for VIP tickets – but fans then found them on resale sites for ten times the price, with some being offered for as much as £7,500. One disappointed fan commented, 'Gutted I missed out on @Adele tickets. Already on resale sites at a five hundred per cent mark up.'

Adele was criticized in the media for the expensive tickets. Other music-lovers were angry even about the less costly tickets, including the £90 ones. On social media, fans branded the ticket price a 'rip off' and one said that spending so much on a concert ticket would be like 'watching money fritter away in a breeze'. Another wrote: 'Adele losing touch with her fans. £90 to stand half a mile away in the open air and see her on a big screen. Crazy.'

However, the cost of staging large musical events had increased across the board. The live music industry was under pressure because, unable to benefit from the furlough scheme, many roadies – lighting and sound technicians – had slipped away into less unpredictable professions. Many companies who provided PA systems and other features of live music had gone bust, and there was a shortage of HGV drivers to move stage gear around. In short, a combination of the pandemic, Brexit and inflation had made staging large shows trickier and more expensive. Adele was not the only artist for whom this was a reality.

Nevertheless, the fuss over her ticket prices proved grist to the mill for those who were keen to take Adele down a notch or two, and portray her as a greedy, grasping woman who had lost all touch with her roots. But the fuss about ticket prices for the Vegas shows was dwarfed entirely by the storm that greeted news that her three-month residency was being postponed. This was to prove the biggest crisis of Adele's career and an earth-shaking moment. Just twenty-four hours before the opening night, she posted a tearful video on social media. 'I'm so sorry, but my show ain't ready,' she told fans in an emotional update on Instagram. 'Half my team have Covid and it's been impossible to finish the show,' she said, adding that 'delivery delays' had also played havoc with her plans.

She said she had been 'awake for thirty hours' trying to

salvage the production, but had simply 'run out of time'. She added that 'it's been impossible to finish the show' and 'I can't give you what I have right now and I'm gutted.' Adele also acknowledged that some fans had already travelled to Las Vegas for the opening weekend. 'I'm sorry, it's last minute. I'm so upset and I'm really embarrassed and I'm so sorry to everyone that's travelled again.' In closing, she vowed: 'We're going to reschedule all the dates, we're on it right now. And I'm going to finish my show. I want to get it to where it's supposed to be [but] we've been up against so much and it just ain't ready.' If there was any hope that her video statement would dampen down controversy over the move, that was soon dashed. The story was dynamite.

The backlash started quickly. Some travelling fans were not in a mood to accept her apologies. Gillian Rowland-Kain said the late cancellation was a 'slap in the face'. She was already on her flight to Las Vegas from New York for the opening night show when she found out about the cancellation via social media. 'I was furious that Adele waited so last minute to make this call,' she said. 'I recognize it's not a call any artist wants to make but she would've known yesterday that the show wouldn't be ready by tomorrow.' Another woman accused Adele of 'crocodile tears' in her Instagram video. Another fan wrote on social media: 'Super bummed that Adele has postponed all of her shows in Las Vegas. I've already spent $1,200 between airfare, hotel, and the concert tickets. Not to mention vacation time from work.'

Questions were quickly raised as to how much in touch with her fans' upset Adele was. Indeed, much of the commentary over the story was predictable in its themes. As the *Daily Telegraph* remarked, 'She is world famous for her supposedly down-to-earth personality, but when you are stationed in a luxury penthouse suite on the 29th floor of Caesar's Palace, it can be hard to keep perspective on how things look from the ground floor. And right now, they look pretty bad.'

A themed merchandise store had already been opened in Caesars Palace and Adele put up a sign, saying: 'Hi guys, I'm so upset to not be with you tonight, but I know some of you are here already, so please hang out and look at the outfits, take pics of anything you want of yourselves and with each other.' It added that anyone who had been due to attend the show could have a complimentary gift from the store, but for some fans the note sounded like an invitation for disappointed fans to share photos of merchandise on social media, effectively asking them to give a spot of free publicity to the 'merch'.

Either way, it was no surprise that this gesture could not assuage the upset and anger felt by many of her fans over what had happened. So, next up, Adele surprised some fans with personal FaceTime calls. During one, she reportedly told a fan: 'You pick a show, I'll cover one of your passes, I'll fly you in to see me on-stage and we'll have a photo together.' However, this was a curious offer to make given that it was not one she was going to be able to extend to everyone hit by the cancellation. Another questionable gesture she offered was free drink tokens to fans who had already arrived in Vegas. This move had to be swiftly cancelled when it transpired that some recipients were under the legal age for the consumption of alcohol. The effort to 'manage' the cancellations seemed scatterbrained and ill thought out compared with the usually closely managed public relations efforts of Team Adele.

Some fans wondered whether they would have a case to sue Adele over the cancellation, but an expert said this was unlikely. Minneapolis attorney Bruce Rivers told *Billboard* magazine that the lengthy terms and conditions fans agree to when purchasing tickets left them little recourse to recover additional travel-related costs in this scenario. As for claims that Adele's apology video opened her up to legal action, Rivers said he doubted her statement exposed her to any real liabilities. Nevertheless, he noted that 'sometimes it's better to let a spokesperson handle these kind of statements' to minimize one's exposure to any threat of future litigation, another indication that the crisis was not being managed well. This suggested that the cancellation may have been every bit as out of the blue as it was presented, offering Adele's team little time at all to work out the deftest way to handle it.

The chorus of criticism began across the Atlantic in the UK. Janet Street-Porter, a regular critic of Adele, branded the singer 'self-obsessed' and said Adele's apology to fans after cancelling her shows was 'snivelling'. She accused her of treating them 'appallingly'. *GB News* presenter Eamonn Holmes said, 'I look at Adele and I think "calm down, it's only a concert, it's only a music show".' Then, as inevitably as ever, Piers Morgan, a regular outspoken critic of Adele, had his say on the story. He reported the 'startling claim' that Adele 'didn't even bother to turn up for on-set rehearsals at Caesars until a few days before the residency was due to start'. He said the 'likely truth' is that Adele 'didn't prepare properly and didn't visit the stage before it was too late – and then threw an extended diva fit of Biblical proportions'. By doing so, he continued, 'she destroyed God knows how many dream trips by die-hard fans who had shelled out not just on tickets, but flights and hotels, too'.

He argued that Adele's 'great gift' used to be her 'rare relatability' to her fans, who 'believed in her because she was a working-class girl who treated them as equals'. Now, he said, 'she has morphed into just another staggeringly rich, privileged, pampered prima donna'. He concluded that 'it would appear health-obsessed Adele's disappeared up her rapidly diminishing celebrity backside', and 'no amount of weeping and wailing can change that very disappointing fact'. As ever, Morgan was outspoken and harsh. One could almost sniff the glee he felt as he criticized Adele yet again. However, his sense of Adele as a 'pampered prima donna' who had lost grasp of her 'rare relatibility' was one shared by a significant number of people. Adele had a growing crisis on her hands.

Indeed, it was perhaps even more devastating for Adele that there was measured criticism from a past champion of hers. 'What has gone wrong on planet Adele?' asked Neil

McCormick in the *Daily Telegraph*. He described the Vegas saga as an 'unmitigated PR disaster', in which 'the finger of blame is starting to shift towards the superstar herself'. He wrote that 'each step of her abject apology seems misjudged' and the entire operation to manage the cancellations was 'haphazard and weirdly unprofessional', he felt. Heaping more criticism, he said that 'the bizarre thing about this whole affair is how unprofessionally it has been handled'.

However, the most stinging part of his commentary was directed at Adele herself. 'The farrago in Vegas makes me wonder if Adele is ascending to the kind of level of fame, ego and power where no one in her team is able to speak honestly to her,' he wrote, adding that 'the word diva is being bandied about'. He said Adele was no longer the 'Tottenham innocent' of the early years of her career; instead, 'she is a super-rich superstar living in the heart of Hollywood'. His sentiments might have been more articulately and kindly expressed than Morgan's, but they were little different in their essence. Moreover, unlike Morgan, McCormick does not put the boot in without a lot of soul-searching first. Morgan will slate anyone for attention, but when you have lost McCormick, you have crossed a line.

As the cancellation made headlines across the globe, there was a tidal wave of speculation over what was behind the dramatic decision. No one, it seemed, was taking Adele's tearful explanation at face value. The *Sun* said that the shows were called off after a 'series of explosive rows' about the staging 'derailed the production'. The tabloid newspaper reported that there were 'behind-the-scenes clashes' with

Adele's set designer Esmeralda Devlin, known as Es. She had previously worked with Adele on her world tour in 2016 but this time things were less harmonious, according to a source who said: 'In spite of the set costing millions to put together, Adele was unhappy with the result, and she made her feelings very clear to Es.'

Another source said Adele made 'endless changes' to the running order and there was 'no real clarity' around what she wanted for the show. 'It seemed that while she has always preferred a stripped-back performance, she was under some pressure to come up with a huge extravaganza,' said the source. 'So there was a constant ricochet between those two versions of what the show should be, and it did cause some quite explosive arguments.' Sources also claimed that 'tension' built up between Adele, her management team and the venue, when the 'perfectionist' singer was asked to perform 'Skyfall' with a sixty-member choir. The *Daily Mail* said that Adele was looking to keep the performance 'low-key' and 'all about the voice'.

However, the difficulties may have been more logistical than that. It had proved difficult to find a venue because so many halls were booked as the concert industry hoped for a full-scale comeback after the disruption of the Covid-19 pandemic. Most venues were already taken by the time Adele's booking agency began searching in 2021 for a venue for her live shows. The deal to stage the shows at the Colosseum at Caesars Palace was only agreed in October 2021, with tickets going on sale in early December. This left the promoters at Live Nation and Adele's production team precious little time to design, perfect and realize the show: approximately eleven weeks to do it all. It may have been that Adele and her team simply took on too much.

The *Sun* claimed that it was a row over a swimming pool that caused the whole thing to fall down. The newspaper reported that Adele had planned to stand in the middle of a pool while performing her songs. However, when she saw the final design for the pool she described it as a 'baggy old pond' and refused, 'point blank', to stand in the middle of it.

For days after her cancellation video, the papers were awash with speculation over what had gone wrong. Much of the coverage was front page news and the story was also chewed over on countless television and radio shows. Social media, too, was dominated by the story. Adele should have been reigning supreme in Vegas, a powerful and deserved reflection of her brilliant fourth album. Instead, she was keeping a low profile, amid headlines about disappointed fans and a 'baggy old pond'.

Over in New York, a celebrity newspaper column suggested that Adele was having a difficult time during rehearsals ahead of the shows. A source said she was 'shouting and sobbing' on the phone while talking to her boyfriend Rich Paul. 'There are rumblings that there are stresses related to Adele's relationship,' said the source. 'I'm told that these stresses caused her to be in a place where she was just not confident moving forward. You can't focus if you're not where you need to be in your head.' A comparison was made with her earlier cancellation of her mini US tour.

As speculation rolled on day after day, some outlets looked back to past statements by Adele about her anxiety over performing live. For instance, in one interview she had said: 'I'm scared of audiences. One show in Amsterdam, I was so nervous I escaped out the fire exit. I've thrown up a couple of times. Once in Brussels, I projectile vomited on someone'. Speaking previously to *Q* magazine, she had said: 'I will not do festivals. The thought of an audience that big frightens the life out of me.'

She has even indicated that she regards live shows as unnatural. 'When I hear artists say "Performing is what I'm meant to do," I think, What? This ain't what you're meant to do. It ain't normal.' Adele is a woman who has expressed significant self-doubt. 'I never love what I do and I don't really rate myself very much,' she said during an interview with US radio in 2010. A year later, in 2011, she said, 'the more successful I get, the more insecurities I'm getting'.

More recently, sources had told the *Daily Mail* that Adele was 'in a panic' before filming her star-studded *Audience With* ... for ITV. A guest told the paper: 'She was freaking out in the dressing room, and this was for an invited audience of friends. The atmosphere was horribly tense. Ben Winston was producing the show and he actually looked as if he was going to be sick from the stress of it.' Could a similar panic attack have derailed the Vegas residency?

Others wondered if Adele was simply anxious about catching Covid and had lost her nerve at the last minute. She had previously told *Rolling Stone* that she would not go on tour because she was worried about the logistics during the pandemic. 'It's too unpredictable, with all the rules and stuff,' she said. 'I don't want anyone coming to my show scared. And I don't want to get Covid, either.' Covid-related hospitalizations in Clark County, Nevada – which encompasses Las Vegas – were approaching the county's record for the pandemic, with 1,872 people hospitalized statewide in the last round of statistics before Adele's dramatic decision. Thirty-seven per cent of people tested were showing a positive Covid result, compared to a seven-day average of just under nineteen per cent in New York City.

Adele's team had put in place significant Covid protocols. The production required ticket-holders to show proof of Covid vaccination, and also produce evidence of a negative Covid test within forty-eight hours of the show. A rapid-test station had been set up near the venue, to handle the influx of those needing on-site testing. However, as she noted in her Instagram video, her tour crew had been hit hard by the rapid spread of the Omicron variant, which prompted a number of competing residency shows at the new Resorts World Las Vegas theatre to tighten their protocols around coronavirus.

The prevailing narrative about the pandemic at the time of the cancellation was to play it down. People were pointing to the comparatively mild experience most had with the Omicron variant and many people felt – perhaps more out of hope than science – that the pandemic was as good as over. However, from Adele's point of view, a virus that attacks the throat was one she would want to avoid whether it came with graver symptoms or not. She was keen to protect her voice, and so any anxiety over a potentially career-ending infection should be understandable.

Of course, if it was a Covid-related panic that played into her decision that would not explain the last-minute nature of the cancellation, and it was that dimension of the story that provoked the most anger and upset. Indeed, it is understood that part of the appeal of a Vegas residency for Adele was that staying in one venue, rather than hitting the road and the skies to move from venue to venue, would reduce the threat of Covid infection.

To try and answer the question everyone was asking, *TMZ* online newspaper reported that 'multiple sources connected to Caesars Palace' said the cancellation had nothing to do with Covid. The sources said that Adele was unhappy with various set pieces, a choir, the sound system and other items associated with the show. She reportedly felt they 'were not good enough'. As the papers continued to speculate over what went wrong, they spoke to other disappointed fans.

Nevertheless, while some fans criticized Adele in the media, there were others who were sympathetic and supportive over her decision to postpone her residency. Adele acknowledged their support on social media. 'I have the best fans in the world!' she wrote. 'Your graciousness and love tonight is overwhelming! Thank you.' Although she had promised to reschedule the dates, the music industry magazine *Billboard*, said this would prove difficult.

An alternative response to the difficulties Adele's team were experiencing with the production was that Adele could have performed a stripped-to-the-basics show. She had toured extensively in the early days with just an acoustic guitar for accompaniment. Her most popular performance was also a simple one: when she was backed by just a piano player at the BRITs for her iconic rendition of 'Someone Like You'. Given that her between-songs patter is also a key part of Adele's appeal – and a dimension of shows that is particularly popular among Vegas audiences – it seemed that she could have put on a show that played to her traditional strengths while the wider set issues were resolved. 'Does Adele really need the kind of everything-and-the-kitchen-sink production usually laid out for autotuned stars who don't have an ounce of her musical talent?' asked the *Daily Telegraph*.

While it felt as if the whole planet was discussing Adele, the lady herself was keeping a relatively low profile. Within hours of her video statement being released, she travelled to Rich Paul's Beverly Hills home. Wearing bedroom slippers and a $450 Louis Vuitton shawl slung over the camo hoodie she had worn when she filmed the message, Adele had taken a Caesars Palace plane to get her out of Vegas and into the arms of her love. Paul's black Mercedes Benz was waiting by the hangar at Van Nuys Airport in the San Fernando Valley, with a driver to whisk her the sixteen miles to his home. A few days later she seemingly sent Paul out to pick up their dinner from Craig's restaurant in West Hollywood.

Then the Vegas story hit the headline again as stage sets were seen being removed from the venue. Next it was announced that Keith Urban, a country music star, would play the hotel's Colosseum theatre on weekends in late March and early April, dashing hopes that Adele would reschedule sooner rather than later.

She was accused of a 'tone-deaf' Instagram post when she made her first full public statement since the cancellation. 'Hiya, so I'm really happy to say that I am performing at the BRITs next week!! Anddddd I'll also be popping in to see Graham for a chat on the couch while I'm in town too,' she wrote, alongside a photograph of her laughing. 'I'm looking forward to it!' she added. 'Oh, and Rich sends his love.' The final sentence of her statement seemed to be a defiant dig at the reporters who had written that her relationship with Rich Paul was on the rocks.

But the statement caused more people to join the 'too big for her boots' camp. As Will Hodgkinson wrote in *The Times*, 'For her fans, coming so soon after the Las Vegas cancellation, Adele flying in from Los Angeles for a glitzy, televised awards show seems just another sign that the working-class girl from Tottenham has become so encased in a bubble of wealth and fame that she is no longer connecting with the people who put her there.'

There was also a sense that mentioning Graham Norton by just his first name in the BRITs announcement added to a feeling that she was only interested in her big-name friends, rather than the ordinary people who made up her fan base and, between them, handed her the massive financial stockpile she enjoyed. She has enjoyed friendships with lots of famous people, as celebrities positively queued up to spend time with her. She has been spotted eating with Jennifer Lawrence and Emma Stone at a Mexican restaurant in Manhattan. Other stars she has hung out with include Robbie Williams, Harry Styles, Rihanna, Nicole Richie and Cameron Diaz. With her name-dropping of Norton and her seeming preference to perform to star-studded audiences, had she, asked Hodgkinson, 'ignored the golden rule when you charge ordinary people a lot of money to see you at Las Vegas: the show must go on'.

Adele had previously commented on how important her fans are to her, saying that 'although I will never meet most of the people who come to see me live, or buy my records, they're part of my life'. The suggestion that she had forgotten about them when she cancelled the Vegas shows will have been incredibly hurtful to her, as well as damaging to her brand. You have to wonder whether the ferocity of the media coverage of the story, going on for weeks as it did, took her by surprise.

The Vegas saga, in its sheer, vast scale, was similar to the fuss caused over Australian reporter Matt Doran's aborted interview with her, in that it reminded us how colossal a story about her can become. While many acts could expect headlines over the Doran and Las Vegas events, few artists would command such a volume and prominence of coverage. Partly through the power and majesty of her voice, partly because of her mammoth popularity, and partly because she was a comparatively reclusive artist who gave the media only limited access to her life, when a story emerged around Adele, it tended to take on a level of significance almost unique to her.

The suggestion that Adele could be 'difficult' was nothing new. As far back as 2016, a BBC journalist said that Adele had been variously described as 'fun, gobby, bolshie, and loud' and 'a big personality who ... is not one to suffer fools'. However, he pointed out that no one in the industry was prepared to say it publicly, demanding instead that their remarks were made off the record. 'They were worried about upsetting the singer, which is not surprising,' wrote the arts commentator Will Gompertz. 'She is a powerful individual who can make people nervous.'

She was, and is, a powerful individual, so nothing could stop the success of 30. In December it was confirmed that the album had landed 2021's official Christmas Number One position. Holding steady at Number One for a fifth consecutive week, with 70,800 chart sales at that stage, 30 had been Adele's second Christmas Number One album; she previously reached the festive top spot in 2015 with her third album 25. Adele was the only artist to exceed one million copies sold in 2021.

All of these measures of success helped her finish 2021 at the top of Bloomberg's Pop Star Power Rankings. Nevertheless, 30 was a relatively modest hit by Adele's standards, and on course to be her lowest-selling album since 19. This should be seen in the context of a wider fall in record sales. When she released 21 in 2011, at least ten albums sold more than one million copies that year, including releases by Lady Gaga, Michael Bublé and Lil Wayne. However, in more recent years, the number of artists who sell albums by that volume has dwindled to just two: Adele and Taylor Swift.

Another sign of her business impact came when she was personally singled out as the cause of a backlog at plants that press vinyl records. A vinyl revival was already underway in the UK before the Covid pandemic however, as lockdowns stopped music fans from going to concerts – or doing much else – the format became even more popular. Within months of the first lockdown, sales of vinyl jumped fifty per cent. This led to pressure at pressing plants. A feature in *The Times* encouraged readers to 'blame Ed Sheeran and Adele' because 'not content with clogging up the charts, the pop superstars have been hogging capacity at already overstretched vinyl pressing plants in the crucial run-up to Christmas'.

According to some reports, Adele completed her third album, *30*, more than six months early to leave time for half a million vinyl copies to be immediately available to fans worldwide. This led to a complaint by her fellow British singer-songwriter, Ed Sheeran, who told an Australian radio station that 'Adele had basically booked out all the vinyl factories, so we had to get a slot.' *The Big Issue* newspaper reported that this led to a backlash from one indie record store in the north-west of England: Ben Savage of Skeleton Records announced that the shop would boycott Adele's new album entirely because the 500,000 pressings ordered had reportedly taken over global vinyl production and delayed releases by other artists by months. 'She's got half a million copies of her album pressed at a time when everybody's struggling to get individual copies pressed,' Savage said.

Rock musician Ian McNabb, one of the acts whose records were pushed back, complained, 'Just because one artist who is obviously a global sensation is releasing an album, does this all mean we've got to sit on the bench and wait six months before we can put anything out?' However, writing for *Billboard*, Lyndsey Havens argued that Adele was being unfairly scapegoated for the vinyl backlog. 'The delays plaguing pressing plants are nothing new,' she noted, 'and surely not caused by Adele or Adele alone, as some reports have insinuated.'

Although an order of an estimated half a million records is 'nothing to scoff at', she added, 'manufacturing delays have been an issue since vinyl demand spiked in July 2020'. Once you throw in problems with supply-chain and labour, plus the shortages of raw materials like PVC and paper products, delays were expected and inevitable, regardless of the popularity of Adele's new release. After all, Havens pointed out, Adele's 500,000 units would amount to less than half a per cent of the total vinyl records manufactured in 2021.

All the same, she maintained her position at the top of the rich list. In May 2021, *The Sunday Times* estimated her net worth to be £130 million. Although this was £20 million down on the previous year, it was still a formidable sum. The newspaper's Rich List report said that a divorce settlement was to blame for the dent in her fortune. Analysis suggested that Adele had earned at least £182 million from touring, songwriting and album sales alone during her career, as of the spring of 2021. This figure is particularly impressive because her catalogue of songs, prior to the release of 30, totalled around fifty – only a 'modest' number.

Rumour has it that she is splashing a fair wedge of that fortune on property. The *South China Morning Post* reported that she was turning two houses in Kensington, London into one 'mega-mansion', spending more than £2 million on the project. It added that she had already dropped coins on property in the US, spending $9.6 million on a house in California. She also bought a house from her long-time friend and neighbour Nicole Richie for $10 million – her third purchase in southern California's Hidden Valley in five years.

Other goodies she has reportedly splashed the cash on include a Porsche Cayenne worth £100,000 as a Christmas gift to herself, and a £15,000 playhouse for Angelo that features three turrets, a picket fence and a veranda, and that can even be hooked up to an electricity supply. The *Sun* said she laid out £20,000 a year on her stylist, Gaelle Paul. None of this helped dispel the feeling among her doubters that Adele had changed and lost sight of her humble charms. However, it should be noted that these critics were outnumbered by those who continued to adore

Adele, regardless of what she spends her riches on. Indeed, for some of her fans, indulgences were part of her charm – the behaviour of a true diva.

She has always had a great strategic mind that has helped the business side of her career. For example, at one point, stories about her started to leak out in the media, so she devised a way to deal with the leaks. At first, she couldn't work out what was happening, but she quickly became suspicious of various members of her inner circle. So, explained Will Gompertz, writing for the BBC, she 'devised a mischievous plan to test the loyalty of her subjects and flush out the treacherous'. She instigated a 'series of private tête-à-têtes with individuals in her court' during which she would 'drop a juicy piece of bespoke insider information'. With the trap duly laid, she would wait to see which, if any, of her 'planted tidbits' found their way into the media. When any did, she would immediately know who the culprit was and they would be swiftly 'excommunicated'. Adele said the project was 'quite fun'.

This sort of trap has since been adopted by other famous people. In 2019, Coleen Rooney, wife of former England football star Wayne Rooney, accused fellow football spouse Rebekah Vardy of leaking Coleen's personal information to British tabloids. Rooney made the incendiary allegation after apparently ensnaring Vardy in an Instagram sting. As footballers' wives and girlfriends are often known as 'Wags', meaning wives and girlfriends, Rooney's detective work became known as 'Wagatha Christie', but Adele was flushing out the leakers before it was fashionable.

Her 'brand' is, mostly, tightly and meticulously managed. Her manager, Jonathan Dickins, once quipped that his job is easy – all he has to do is spend ninety-nine per cent of his time saying 'No'. The BBC described her as 'one of the world's biggest entertainment brands, right up there with Grand Theft Auto, Star Wars, FIFA 2016, and Call of Duty'. Tim Ingham, who runs the much-watched website Music Business Worldwide, said her commercial clout is that of a 'freak'. A high-ranking music executive called Adele 'an anomaly', 'label-proof' and a beacon 'of hope for the industry'. How she, and her 'brand', recover from the dent that the Vegas scandal inflicted on her reputation will determine whether she builds that brand even higher in the future, or whether the cancellation will leave an indelible stain on her career.

Then there are the musical questions. Having left a three-year gap between her first two albums, she left four years between albums two and three, and then a five-year gap between her third and fourth collections. So it would be optimistic to expect significant new material anytime soon. A criticism rightly levelled at her when 30 came out was that it contained so few surprises in terms of style. Perhaps the only time her music has genuinely surprised anyone was on track two of 25, the poppy 'Send My Love (To Your New Lover)'. Other than that, remarked a critic, Adele's music 'breaks less ground than a pneumatic drill made from plasticine'. Can she move beyond the beautiful, yet narrow, group of singers she has been influenced by? Does she want to?

Possibly an even bigger question is whether this astonishing woman, who has composed and sung heartbreak anthems adored across the globe, can find lasting romantic happiness.

There was much hullabaloo when she went out in public for the first time with her new boyfriend, the sports agent Rich Paul. Born in 1981, Paul grew up in Cleveland, USA. He founded Klutch Sports Group, which represents a number of leading NBA (National Basketball Association) players, in addition to NFL (National Football League) players in more recent years. He and Adele rolled up to Game 5 of the 2021 NBA Finals – the Phoenix Suns versus the Milwaukee Bucks – and sat in the stands with one of Paul's clients, LeBron James. Adele and Paul had been friends for a while before anything turned romantic. 'He was always there, I just didn't see him,' she told *Vogue*. She admitted she was 'a bit drunk' when they first met. 'I said: "Do you want to sign me? I'm an athlete now."' It seemed a shared love of humour was one of the things they first bonded over – that and dancing. 'He's just so fucking funny,' she said. 'He was dancing. All the other guys were just sitting around. He was just dancing away.'

She didn't enjoy dating before she met Paul – she described the process as 'shit'. But then, just before her dad died, 'Rich just incredibly arrived,' she told *Vogue*. He brought with him a sense of safety and security. 'I don't feel anxious or nervous or frazzled,' she said. 'It's quite the opposite. It's wild.' She felt she was in control, though. 'I'm a thirty-three-year-old divorced mother of a son, who's actually in charge,' she said. 'The last thing I need is someone who doesn't know where they're at, or what they want. I know what I want. And I really know what I don't want.' She added, 'I just love being around him. I just love it.'

In January 2022, they were spotted at a basketball game between the Lakers and the Atlanta Hawks in Los Angeles. The *Daily Mail* said the singer was seen 'laughing up a storm' next to Paul as the couple watched the game at the Crypto. com Arena. She was wearing a pair of black and white Nike Air Force 1 trainers, with a pair of gold hoop earrings. Her footwear prompted *Harper's Bazaar* magazine to comment that she 'may be becoming a sneakerhead'. The *Sun* said Adele looked in fine spirits, adding that she 'couldn't stop laughing'.

In the same month, the couple popped out for dinner at the Italian eatery Giorgio Baldi in Santa Monica. Adele and Paul continued to grab the attention of the media every time they stepped out on the town as the world opened up following the strictest lockdowns.

As we have seen, some publications claimed that Adele had cancelled the Vegas residency due to difficulties between her and Paul. 'There's trouble in paradise,' one report cited an inside source as saying. 'That's why she can't perform.' It was also claimed that she was desperately trying to 'fix' their relationship.

But can she fix her relationship with the fans she upset with her Vegas cancellation? Will those who fell in love with Adele because they thought 'there's someone like me' be able to continue relating to a woman who splashes fortunes on expensive treats for herself, and lets them down at the last moment after they've spent their savings on travelling to see her in person?

Perhaps they will look a little deeper and find that Adele is still the same as them? What seems clear when you explore her life story is that the pressures of fame and showbusiness are unsettling for Adele. Behind her sassy, defiant persona and far beyond that heavenly voice lurks a sensitive woman for whom the combined pressures of everyday life and celebrity are a real challenge.

To continue rendering heartbreak with such authenticity, vulnerability and emotional dexterity only adds to the pressure on Adele. If she were simply miming meaningless pop tat, written by a third party, her existence would be so much easier, but then she wouldn't mean so much to everyone. If she was in a pop band she would be able to keep a low profile when she wasn't 'feeling it'. These options aren't there for a solo star with a voice like Adele's.

People keep asking what happened to that humble girl from Tottenham, but the truth is that she is still there, it's just that the circus around her kept getting bigger and bigger. For a robotic or cynical personality, that process would be simpler, but for Adele it has proven a challenge and one that she hasn't always been able to respond to perfectly. Why? Because she is human, because she is, still, someone like you.

ACKNOWLEDGEMENTS

Thanks as ever to the folk at Michael O'Mara Books, especially Louise Dixon, Meredith MacArdle and Rowena Anketell. Thanks also to Judith Palmer and Natasha Le Coultre for leaving no stone unturned.

BIBLIOGRAPHY

There are countless newspapers and magazines I have used for my research on this amazing woman, all credited within the text.

Adele, Sean Smith, HarperCollins, 2016
Adele: The Biography, Chas Newkey-Burden, John Blake, 2012
Adele: A Celebration of an Icon and Her Music, Welbeck Publishing, 2012
Someone Like Adele, Caroline Sanderson, Omnibus, 2012

DISCOGRAPHY

ALBUMS
19 (XL, 2008)
21 (XL, 2011)
25 (XL, 2015)
30 (Columbia, 2021)

SINGLES
'Hometown Glory' (XL, 2007)
'Chasing Pavements' (XL, 2008)
'Cold Shoulder' (XL, 2008)
'Make You Feel My Love' (XL, 2008)
'Rolling In The Deep' (XL, 2010)
'Someone Like You' (XL, 2011)
'Set Fire to the Rain' (XL, 2011)
'Rumour Has It' (XL, 2011)
'Turning Tables' (XL, 2011)
'Skyfall' (XL, 2012)
'Hello' (XL, 2015)
'When We Were Young' (XL, 2016)
'Send My Love (To Your New Lover)' (XL, 2016)
'Water Under the Bridge' (XL, 2016)
'Easy on Me' (Columbia, 2021)
'Oh My God' (Columbia, 2021)

PICTURE CREDITS

Page 1: Dave Etheridge-Barnes/Getty Images (top);
JMEnternational/Getty Images (centre);
Andre Csillag/Shutterstock (bottom).

Page 2: Kevin Mazur/WireImage/Getty Images (top);
John Shearer/WireImage/Getty Images (bottom).

Page 3: Jeff Kravitz/FilmMagic/Getty Images (top);
Andy Sheppard/Redferns/Getty Images (bottom).

Page 4: Dave M. Benett/Getty Images (top);
Kevin Mazur/WireImage/Getty Images (bottom).

Page 5: Kevork Djansezian/Getty Images (top);
Christopher Polk/Getty Images for NARAS (bottom).

Page 6: Jeff Kravitz/FilmMagic/Getty Images (top);
WPA Pool/Getty Images (bottom).

Page 7: Luca Teuchmann/WireImage/Getty Images (top);
Andy Buchanan/AFP via Getty Images (centre);
Morne de Klerk/Getty Images (bottom).

Page 8: Karwai Tang/WireImage/Getty Images.

INDEX